# GENIUS
## AN IDEOLOGY IN LITERATURE

# GENIUS

## AN IDEOLOGY IN LITERATURE

*by*

Robert Currie

1974

CHATTO & WINDUS

LONDON

Published by
Chatto & Windus Ltd
42 William IV Street
London WC2N 4DF

\*

Clarke, Irwin & Co Ltd
Toronto

ISBN 7011 2014 2

Printed in Great Britain by
Cox & Wyman Ltd
London, Fakenham and Reading

# CONTENTS

Page

FOREWORD 9

INTRODUCTION 15

CHAPTER 1: *The One and the Many in Romanticism*

The crisis of ideology 25
The realm of alienation 29
The transcendental enterprise 37
Problems of genius 45

CHAPTER 2: *Hoffmann's Theory of Genius*

The estranged world and the alienated self 56
The musical-erotic paradise 62
Genius and philistines 70
Genius, suffering and martyrdom 80

CHAPTER 3: *Kierkegaard and the Romantic Crisis*

The present age 88
The tyranny of normality 97
Existential genius 103
Existentialism and philistinism 110

CHAPTER 4: *The Modernism of Wyndham Lewis*

Philistia 116
Split self and puppet man 121
Inimical genius 128
Visions of death and hell 135

CHAPTER 5: *Kafka and the Defeat of Genius*

The urban world 143
The sexual underworld 150

# CONTENTS

The realm of significance                                155
Genius as victim                                         168

CHAPTER 6: *Beckett's Transcendental Nihilism*

The world of habit                                       171
The failure of knowledge                                 176
Existence and non-existence                              182
Nihilism and non-expression                              189

CHAPTER 7: *The Ideology of Genius*

From romanticism to modernism                            194
The triumph of philistinism                              201
Culture without genius                                   209
Alienation and democracy                                 214

# FOREWORD

THIS is a study of ideology, that is, of ideas used for ulterior purposes. The chief example of ideology here analysed is the notion of *genius* as it has developed in modern Europe. 'Genius' may signify a quality or a power, and one who possesses that quality or power. This book examines both meanings of the word, but concentrates upon the relationship between the person of genius and the larger concept of *alienation* because, according to the ideology of genius, *humanity needs genius to rescue it from alienation.*

One sense in which the word 'alienation' can be used derives from a general pattern of thought which has been applied as a reactionary ideology especially during the two hundred years since the appearance of Rousseau's major works and the period of the *Sturm und Drang*, or 'Age of genius'. However this concept of alienation has been defined, it always includes the propositions that *the self is divided from the self* and that *the self is divided from the world.* These propositions establish the universality of the concept of alienation, because the mind seems to reflect upon itself and upon the world as *objects* and, therefore, as things separated—'alienated'—from itself.

The commonplace inference from these propositions, the inference which makes the concept of alienation

9

ideologically so efficacious, is the inference that *the divisions which we experience should be overcome, and would be overcome in a higher realm*. In my view this inference is neither necessary nor desirable. I cannot accept that our condition requires us, or permits us, to oppose to it the idea of another and a better condition, whatever that idea's utility as a stimulus to beneficial social change.

Nor can I accept two further propositions contained within the concept of alienation considered as the foundation for the ideology of genius, namely, *that the present alienated world is divided into the one and the many* and that *the higher realm will be introduced through the one*. These propositions are very persuasive. Each of us is a one, an individual, who tends to set greatest value upon himself; upon his personal individuality; and therefore upon the general idea of individuality. Furthermore, most people conclude that great individuals have played a decisive part in shaping society, religion, art and science, and that the one in this sense is much more valuable than the many.

I am ready to admit the significance of great individuals, and the magnitude of their contribution to human affairs; and I cannot deny that the idea of the one, no less than the idea of another and a better condition, has roused ambitious men to great achievements. Yet I wish to argue that the concept of alienation has been employed precisely to condemn achievements, both of great individuals and of the many who constitute the mass of mankind. For ideas about alienation and about genius have been used most often in reaction to the mass power mobilised through spread of education, growth of cities, capitalism, liberalism, constitutionalism and democracy: each of which developments is partly the work of great individuals. Such mass power has brought intellectuals opposed to it, sometimes not unjustifiably, to interpret their world as a condition of alienation and to seek to transcend it in a higher realm to be realised through the work of genius.

This analysis assumes that our culture has become predominantly secular; that romanticism is the first great phase of secular culture—to which phase very largely we still belong; but also that romanticism is, in T. E. Hulme's words, 'spilt religion'. Because romanticism inherits and secularises the religious world view, I introduce my discussion of romanticism by briefly examining that world view as it appears in Judaism and in Christianity. But neither subject is central to my argument and, though this book has in a sense a religious theme, that theme is worked out from material either wholly or chiefly secular in character.

The analysis also assumes that, although romanticism developed from the decline of Christianity (a decline quite irrespective of the truth or falsity of Christian doctrine), and invaded every area of culture, especially between 1750 and 1850, romanticism too declined in favour of another epoch of thought, which I have called *modernism*. Modernism developed from romanticism—just as romanticism developed from Christianity—but kept at least as much of romanticism as romanticism kept of Christianity.

For the particular purposes of this book I have interpreted Christianity as a *religious* understanding of alienation and its transcendence in a higher realm. Romanticism thus appears as a *secular* understanding of alienation and its transcendence, which retained most of Christianity's optimism about the possibility of a higher order. Modernism differs from romanticism, according to my definition, not so much in its basic categories as in the *pessimism* with which it understands these categories. A romantic posits a higher order which is, in general estimation, a better world, and which can be attained. A modernist doubts, almost to the point of disbelief, that the higher order can be attained; and he interprets the higher order in terms so ascetic, or even so objectionable, as to repel all but those who can rise to the austerity of his creed.

I have tried to analyse romantic and modernist interpretations of alienation and of genius above all as they appear in literature: this is mainly a book of literary criticism. About three-quarters of the book examines in detail the work of five authors: Hoffmann, Kierkegaard, Lewis, Kafka and Beckett. These are certainly not the only critics to have employed the concepts of alienation and of genius. But they are among the most important of such critics, and together they form a group which—while by no means amounting to a school—has many inter-connections.

They are also men of considerable influence. Kafka and Kierkegaard have a significance which is unlikely to be disputed. Beckett seems to me to be the foremost living writer in western Europe. Hoffmann and Lewis are much less familiar, at least in Britain. But in German prose of the romantic period, Hoffmann stands second only to Goethe. He is a theoretician who deeply influenced both Kierkegaard and Marx— whose unfinished novel *Skorpion and Felix* is overtly indebted to Hoffmann. He is also a novelist and short story writer, the chief of whose numerous disciples is Dostoevsky; and he is a musician and musical critic who has inspired, among others, Schumann, Wagner and Tchaikovsky. Lewis, who drew heavily upon Hoffmann in his literary work, is the most important painter and (especially for artists) the most significant art critic, in twentieth-century England. Though one of the leading few writers in English since 1900, Lewis has been almost ignored by scholars up till the last ten years. But the increasing interest in both Hoffmann and Lewis suggests the persistence of the ideology of genius.

# INTRODUCTION

THE ideology of genius assumes that the self exists in a condition where it and the world are foreign to itself; where the lower values of multiplicity and division have overcome the higher values of unity; and where man's very humanity is fragmented and lost. Man must therefore strive to establish, over against this lower order, a higher order in which alienation is transcended, in which unity is achieved or restored, and in which humanity is fully realised.

The proper agency of man's struggle for unity is whatever, in the present condition of alienated multiplicity, comes closest to unity. What approximates to the one in the world of the many—some great historic individual, for example—is expected to conquer alienation and introduce the higher order, even though that individual continues, until the higher order is introduced, to suffer division and alienation within himself.

This ideology begins in various places. Jewish doctrines of creation and fall, for example, presume the unity and goodness of God and the evil multiplicity of man. According to these doctrines man is created as a plurality; he is inferior because he is merely a creature; and he has sinned through disobedience. Expulsion from the garden of Eden symbolises alienation in this essentially static picture of man's condition.

The dynamic element in Jewish theology is the doctrine of the Messiah or Christ. The Messiah was a royal, angelic figure who would come from God, conquer the evil multiplicity of the world, bring history to a close and introduce by force a unified realm of perfection, a new Eden. Although the Messiah was the instrument of God, endowed with divine grace and authority, he was nevertheless a man, a great historic individual. The Messiah was the one in the world of the many. He was a genius who possessed the greatest human powers, yet drew further powers from God, a natural, but mysterious and even, humanly speaking, irrational source. The Messiah prefigured the unity and perfection of the transcendental realm itself but also represented the alienated condition, being from and of God but simultaneously from and of man. Alienation entered the Messiah's being, and he could escape from alienation only when, through him, the world's alienation was ended.

Judaism refused to find the Messiah in any one historical figure. Christianity did identify the Messiah with the historical Jesus of Nazareth. The new religion's central doctrine was man's salvation from present estrangement in sin and weakness: and Christ was the agency of this salvation. Moreover, Christianity offered not salvation in the present order but transcendence of the present order in a higher realm.

Christianity agreed with Judaism in admitting the genius's alienation during the interim before his work was completed, and explained this alienation by arguing that the transcendental personality was at once both fully man and fully God. The God-man Jesus Christ, like the Jewish Messiah, would forcibly conquer evil; but Christ's adversary was an abstract and universal state of evil, rather than the purely concrete and historical forces against which the Jewish Messiah was expected to fight.

Furthermore, Christ's victory, unlike the Messiah's, was to be achieved in two modes. Like the Messiah, Christ as hero, the perfect God-man victorious, would destroy evil multiplicity by violence; but unlike the Messiah, Christ as martyr, God-man defeated and divided, would triumph through suffering and crucifixion.

Christian theology interacted with Greek and Near Eastern cultures. Neo-Platonism, which greatly influenced the development of Christianity, attributed the world to one creative absolute whence power emanated, through the successive agencies of pure intelligence, the soul of the world, the souls of men and the souls of animals, and finally lost itself in matter. This system proposed to transcend the estrangement between the absolute idea and matter, between the one and the many, through the unity of philosophical understanding. The Manichaeans taught that light, the creative force, issued from the goodness and unity of the deity through a series of stages, ever more weakly, into the evil, multiplicity and darkness of matter. Christ and Mani, the founder of Manichaeism, shared a transcendental work in which the Manichaean believer would participate when he subdued in himself the estranging darkness of matter and evil.

Augustine of Hippo was in turn a Manichaean, a Neo-Platonist and a Christian. As a Manichaean, Augustine admitted the dualism essential to the concept of alienation; as a Neo-Platonist, he understood evil to be estrangement or division from God; and as a Christian, he taught Christ's supreme transcendental work and the believer's mystical participation in that work. Augustinian and later Christian mysticism prepared for both the reformation doctrine of faith and the idea of secular genius: the former by claiming that the believer's mystical communion with God transcended alienation; and the latter by assuming that, to achieve this transcendence, the mystic must possess great human qualities and the mysterious power of God within him.

But mystical transcendence remained quite secondary to the church's routine activities. For, while fulfilling its many cultural, social and political tasks, the church translated the ideology of alienation into organisational terms. The alienated condition was interpreted as the work of diabolical forces which, however, manifested themselves in human life not through great historic acts but in prosaic breaches of ethical and social codes. The universal transcendental agency remained the person and work of the hero-martyr Christ; but that agency operated through the papacy which acted as an *institutional* transcendental personality, whose power developed *ex officio* like that of the Roman emperors whom the popes succeeded.

The papacy's institutional transcendentalism profoundly influenced European culture. The pope was an organisational genius, whose office gave him earthly sovereignty, and divine authority to overcome human estrangement, and who thus originated the far reaching claims of absolute monarchy, and of certain modern political systems. The organisation of the church consolidated the hierarchical element in the concept of the one and the many.

A slow rise in living standards and the growth of cities created, during the later middle ages, the social conditions in which Christianity could develop certain tendencies contrary to this essentially static and authoritarian system. Christian mysticism, though an *élitist* tradition, became more widely understood through successive vulgarisations which suggested, not that just some few men, but that man in general could transcend his own estrangement through mystical experience. Furthermore, the church's ritual system, despite priestly restrictions upon it, also annulled the alienation from God of whomever should duly receive the sacraments. Hence both mysticism and sacrament facilitated the reformation, which replaced ritual by a faith which extended and generalised the principles of mysticism.

The reformation secularised the concept of alienation. The doctrine of justification by faith revealed, in those who truly knew and believed in God, power to achieve a psychical transcendence hitherto reserved to mystics. The otherness of the higher realm, guarded by the mystical *élite* and made concrete in the sacrament, now gave way to an inner action of knowledge and belief which, because it was available to all men, encouraged the secular notion that by mental effort man can overcome his own estrangement. In contrast to Judaism and to traditional Christianity, according to which transcendence of alienation was ultimately reserved to God, the reformation gave man transcendental power and, in a sense, made him god.

Yet the reformation also intensified man's sense of alienation. It denied him the certainty of the church's tradition, ritual and organisation, and so emphasised his separation and weakness. Moreover the reformation required man to rest his salvation upon knowledge and belief—that is, upon the workings of mind—and therefore exacerbated the epistemological problems which made doubt so important an element in European culture.

The reformation's democratic tendencies complemented these tendencies to secularism. The pre-reformation church's hierarchy, and its sacramental system, had maintained principles of authority and inequality in the sphere of man's chief concerns. All men were held to exist in a condition of alienation: but from this condition the priesthood was, so to speak, exempted by its peculiar powers, which the laity needed in order to transcend their own estrangement through the sacraments.

The doctrine of the priesthood of all believers destroyed these principles because it dispensed with priestly mediation between man and God. The reformation thus introduced the modern concept of democracy since, just as faith in the end equates man with God, in the end it equates all men with each other.

And in this way, too, the reformation intensified men's sense of alienation. For its democratic tendencies emancipated the many from the controls of a world formerly at least *apparently* unitary, and fragmented society into separate, more or less free, individuals.

If the reformation thus rendered transcendence of alienation the more urgent, it also changed the concept of the transcendental agency. Reformation theology taught that alienation was to be overcome, not through the routine of the church, but through human activity in history. As soon as the transcendental lay within the sphere of men's knowledge and belief, that man who knew most, who believed most—and who brought most to the knowledge and belief of other men—could be identified as the secular, the historical transcendental personality: that is, he could be identified as genius.

Luther, above all, fulfilled men's new expectations of transcendental personality, and so stands as the first example of genius in the reformation era of secularism and democracy. Like genius, Luther was a man of supreme human qualities, who possessed also a mysterious suprahuman power. Part monk, part secular clergyman, part Catholic, part Protestant, part saint, part vulgarian, Luther manifested the alienated consciousness common to every man but perhaps acutely present in genius as the greatest, the most human, of men. Like genius, moreover, Luther constructed an entire new order. For he broke the power of a church now accused of alienating men from God; established a new religious movement; created new states and new politics; and promised all his followers the salvation for which men longed.

Secular messianism could not stop at Luther. Since faith made all men equal, all men could aspire to genius. The idea of genius therefore gave rise to numerous imitation Luthers, each with their own doctrines, practices and followers. Such men seemed to negate whatever unity the church had once maintained, and Luther sought to preserve; and their shortcomings seemed to mock the very idea of genius as Luther had renewed it. These men, in religion, politics, or art, have been termed *philistines*, a usage made familiar in English by Arnold's attack upon bourgeois liberals and nonconformists.

The Biblical Philistines are enemies of the truth vouchsafed to the Israelites. Modern philistines are those who, according to their critics, oppose transcendental aspirations and transcendental personality. The philistines divide mankind and vindicate the principle of the many. Indeed they degrade and stultify the only means whereby alienation may be transcended: for a thousand prophets make even the one true prophet ridiculous. The philistines are imitative, false, partial, narrow, commonplace and divisive. They ape genius and they perpetuate alienation.

The conviction that man was divided within and without increased when the reformation brought religious war. The era when men's transcendental aspirations had been contained within the institutional routine of a long-established, catholic church now seemed an age of unity, order and authority, rather than of false doctrine and repression of the mind. But neither the advocates of counter-reformation nor their Protestant opponents succeeded in forming new structures of ecclesiastical authority. Instead they created, in absolute monarchy, a more or less secular representation of the pre-reformation church's system of organisational transcendentalism. The absolutist programme was the conquest of the divisions caused by the reformation. Absolute monarchy must end its subjects' fragmentation, and to do so must realise, within the routine of its own organisation, the concept of the one as secular transcendental agency.

Because the absolute monarch was to be a genius, he must claim the powers and character of genius: hence King James told his son that God 'made you a little god to sit on His throne and rule over men'. And because absolutism must create and preserve political unity, the absolutist kingdom had to be interpreted as a secular, institutional, and this-worldly version of the kingdom of heaven, a claim rather more difficult to substantiate than those long advanced, for example, in favour of the church.

In any event, absolutism's geographical, and hence political and cultural, limitations were determined in the first half of the seventeenth century. In 1648 the treaty of Westphalia ended the Thirty Years' War and confirmed the establishment of absolute monarchy in France, Germany and Scandinavia. In 1649 the execution of King Charles revealed the futility of the Stuart bid to establish absolutism in Britain. The continent and the islands went their own ways.

# I

## THE ONE AND THE MANY
## IN ROMANTICISM

### *The crisis of ideology*

ALL things become political things and politics become universal once men so desire unity that they require state and society to arise from, and in turn to express, the one inner truth of existence. Men so disposed seek a government which will transcend their alienation from true humanity. And the first governments of this kind were the absolutist monarchies which, as prototypes of much subsequent government, and of a whole ideal of government, posed many problems fundamental to modern politics and culture.

Absolutism's first task was to halt religious war by re-establishing the unity of one religion, or at least of one state religion. This task was successfully completed. Absolutism's second and much more complex task was to prevent recurrence of civil disorder by securing the citizens' absolute loyalty to absolutism itself.

Before the reformation few men were taught to experience either political or religious faith, and therefore few felt need of such faith to justify and motivate their outward compliance in the contemporary governmental or ecclesiastical system. Men did not then demand of government—or of secular life generally— the evidences of a transcendental order which, for many centuries, they were content to seek in the

25

church. After the reformation, men tended to adopt the secular logic of reformation teaching and sought secular satisfaction of the desire for personal convictions which the reformation had aroused. Absolutism responded by presenting the absolute monarch as secular genius who would introduce a political earthly paradise.

No doubt absolutism's transcendental power was questioned only belatedly if at all by the monarchy itself, its immediate partisans, theoreticians and beneficiaries. These last were indeed many. For the absolutist bureaucracy's increasing demands for lawyers and clerks, created an ever-expanding legal-administrative bourgeoisie dependent upon the monarchy.

But even these new bourgeois groups included some who doubted the state's claims. The objective character of absolutism strengthened such doubts. The growth of nationalism encouraged absolutist governments in an aggressive and bellicose policy of expansion. Lack of consensus within the state, administrative exigencies, and the legacy of intolerance from reformation and pre-reformation society, brought absolute monarchy towards a tyranny rendered the more objectionable by the evident personal deficiencies of certain monarchs.

Life in absolutist society could not always compensate for absolutist politics. Extended education produced a quality of culture which seemed to compare unfavourably with the standards of the past. Increased economic, administrative and military efficiency rested on a sub-division of labour which appeared to divide man into skills or aptitudes. Rationalist science seemed to fragment human consciousness into separate faculties, such as reason and feeling, and to reduce man's powers by discovering irreversible natural laws to which man was alleged to be subject.

Those whom such things offended found no comfort in the British alternative to absolutism. Continental knowledge of Britain was drawn chiefly from books such as Voltaire's *Philosophical Letters* and Adam Smith's *An Enquiry into the Nature and Causes of the Wealth of Nations*. Voltaire, Smith and other writers agreed that the British were men whose independence bordered on anarchy; who divided religion into self-governing sects, and politics into unruly factions and parties; who favoured unlimited division of labour and uncontrolled commercial competition; and who pursued scientific enquiry without regard for authority, tradition, or higher values. Britain served continental critics either as a yardstick by which to measure the deficiencies of absolute monarchy, or as a paradigm of democracy's dangers. But Britain could not satisfy these critics' demands for a new model of human and social life.

Nor could the American or French revolutions (in part these critics' work) provide the model which they sought. America seemed remote and outlandish: admirable, if at all, in its vastness and boldness, as a monument to human endeavour; terrible, in its barbarity and materialism, as an example of the feebleness of human achievement, especially without the aid of the latest social and political theory.

France was well supplied with such theory. But

France was a partial encouragement only. Revolutionary methods, especially the reign of terror, commended themselves to certain extremists, who nevertheless condemned the outcome of revolution as mere bourgeois republicanism. Napoleon did seem to embody the ideal of genius as had few men before him, yet his personality and policy ultimately denied him the wholehearted allegiance of critics of the *ancien régime*.

These practical disappointments convinced certain European thinkers that their criticism alone displayed the reality of the present order, and that their ideals alone revealed the true goal of the future. These thinkers, estranged from absolutism and from the political systems that succeeded it, created—often from precedents in absolutist theory, from rationalist science and philosophy—the principles and much of the practice of romanticism.

Romantics held man to be alienated, not from God in whom by and large they had ceased to believe, but from nature, or from history, which came to take God's place. The present estranging order was said to deny man his natural or historical self and to cut him off from the natural or historical world which, therefore, appeared alien, constricting and menacing. 'Man was born free, and he is everywhere in chains', ruled Rousseau.

Hence man must be restored to the freedom in which his true humanity consists. He must transcend his alienation; and, according to most romantics, he must do so through the work of a supreme although—

for the duration of that work—still alienated human individual. This individual was the genius, the one among the many, who (unlike the many) could already call up something of that force which would preponderate in the higher realm that he would introduce.

Such is romantic perfectionism: perhaps the reward of the many, certainly the work of the one who would triumph through force, either directly as hero or, in a paradox whose pessimism already 'modernises' romanticism, as martyr. Once genius had triumphed, his own and the world's alienation would cease and a realm of unity and perfection would be established.

## The realm of alienation

Romantic criticism of contemporary humanity's alienated condition derived much of its force from its notion of early, and especially classical man. The ancient Greeks, the romantics believed, enjoyed a free, harmonious and integral existence. According to the Hellenic ideal, in Pater's words, 'Man is at unity with himself, with his physical nature, with the outward world'. But man is no longer so. 'Little we see in Nature that is ours', complained Wordsworth of the modern life of 'Getting and spending':

—Great God! I'd rather be
A Pagan suckled in a creed outworn. . . .

Schiller's theory of the 'naïve' world of immediacy

and unity, now necessarily lost, though surviving in genius—the strange and uncouth child of nature—complements both romantic antiquarianism and Wordsworth's lyrical vision. Man had been, especially in classical antiquity, and indeed might be again (but not in the alienated present) one and harmonious with himself and with nature.

He who did exist in the present was held to be utterly divided within himself. Some regarded the mind as a bundle of perceptions, altogether lacking the unity and identity once attributed to individual personal intelligence. Unified man, commanding the natural world as he commanded his own limbs, gave way to a divided man whose very self was invaded by the natural forces that manipulated him. Kant's ethical theories divided human personality into two selves, the noumenal self which existed, if only as an ideal, in the world of thought, a 'proper self', towards which man could strive; and a phenomenal self in the world of sense, where, however, man was 'only an appearance of himself'.

But however he was analysed, alienated man was held to encounter all the dangers of an anarchy that perhaps found its fullest expression in Schopenhauer's theory of the will, a turbulent lower power which threatened to extinguish the self in a chaos of drives and instincts. The psychological interpretation of man's alienated condition as an anarchy in which self was divided from self could be complemented, more-over, by a sociology that found man to be estranged in, yet from, a turbulent, anarchic social world.

England was the prime example of such a world. Thus Shelley, more or less from the left, condemned his England in a poem called 'The Mask of Anarchy'; while Arnold, more or less from the right, attacked his England, fifty years later, in his book *Culture and Anarchy*. *Laissez faire* political economists, moreover, often described British commercial life as a system in which each individual pursued his own economic ends, regardless of any man but—according to critics—in the end destroying all. These commentators believed that out of this disorder came the best of all orders, in which perfect competition maximised efficiency, and hence happiness. But continental writers, who lacked such optimism, took a much gloomier view of British commercialism.

Hegel, for example, drew from the political economists the concept of 'bourgeois' or 'civil' society, that is, the society in which the disorderly conflict of anarchic men is unregulated by the unity of a state such as Hegel advocated. 'Civil society is the battlefield of the individual private interests of all against all', wrote Hegel. And such 'division' and 'particularity' distorted man and estranged him from his ideal universality.

Revolution could destroy human values in a disorder as estranging as that of bourgeois economics. Herder's *Yet Another Philosophy of History for the Enlightenment of Man*, which appeared in 1774, warned that the 'fundamentals of humanity' were 'depleted' as lower classes displaced the higher, only to become worse than they had been. Order and authority had gone, claimed

Herder, leaving only an anarchy dignified by the slogan of liberty, fraternity and equality, which would cause 'a thousand evils to be committed'. The reign of terror, an event which, according to Schiller, plunged a whole century into 'barbarism and slavery', justified Herder's fears.

Such crises could be interpreted as those historical moments in which, as Herder put it, 'destiny re-wound the giant run-down clock' of humanity—not without much noise and disturbance. But most eighteenth-century critics used the clock to symbolise the realm of alienation not as a dynamic but as a static system, a perpetual motion machine in which men were cogs. As cog in a machine, man is estranged both into an *object*, a cog, and into an *instrument*, a means to the transmission of power. For, in the clockwork society, all men become employees and their life and their labour are divided into operations ever more restricted and isolated.

Rousseau's doctrine of the incompatibility of trade and creative integrity contrasts transcendental man with the life of the cog in the machine. The issue was debated by the young Wilhelm Meister. 'The poet is at once teacher, prophet, friend of gods and of men', he told his friend Werner. 'Do you want him to descend to some miserable job?'

Attempts to escape the life of the social machine were unlikely to succeed: as indeed *Wilhelm Meister* seems to show. Jobs were now everywhere. 'The relationship of master and servant is the most prevalent characteristic of our public offices, of the trades and of all social orders, from peasant to minister of state, and from minister to priest', wrote Herder.

That man should serve man was by no means uncommon before the eighteenth century. But perhaps it was this century that first enabled the relatively poor to entertain aspirations as sharply at variance with their status as those entertained, on behalf of 'man', by romantic critics. On the other hand, perhaps even in the eighteenth century, the relatively poor cared less about such privations than did their apparent champions. Certainly these critics and their successors found in the subordinations caused by employment an estrangement not much complained of by those more accustomed to employment.

Schiller saw alienated man as less even than a subordinate. His *Aesthetic Education of Man* argues that rigorous differentiation of offices and occupations in the ever more complex 'clockwork of the state' severs 'the inward union of human nature'. Society measures man by his work and defines him only by that skill or ability which makes him employable—while as man he disappears from view. Furthermore, because such a cog in the machine is required to work only at, and as, a fragment of the great administrative or productive whole, it becomes a fragment itself; and the totality of that fragment's existence corresponds merely to its gainful occupation, whose stamp upon alienated personality displaces the stamp of humanity.

The man is the job, as Marx argued when, recapitulating Schiller's analysis half a century later, he interpreted the worker in contemporary capitalist production as a human machine, endowed with a life-sustaining belly, and exercising the 'abstract activity' of a specialised technique of labour. Schiller's bureaucratic cog has become Marx's cotton-working cog, a different employee who, nevertheless, suffers the same alienation.

But Marx expressed this notion in new ways. Ludwig Feuerbach had argued that man alienated his true self in the fantasy of a 'God' who was really man. Applying the same argument to economics, Marx discovered man's essential humanity in hypotases such as money or labour. The labourer, according to Marx, was his labour, and capitalism was a mechanical, estranging order of society which extracted labour from the labourer as the price of his survival. The labourer was therefore alienated not only because his personality was suppressed or distorted in order to develop mere job skills, but also because his job abstracted and extorted from him the substance of his self, which thereafter existed only as something estranged from and foreign to him. '*I am nothing*', Marx held alienated man to say, '*and I should be everything*'.

Unfortunately, however, estrangement into the fragmented many made man into the denizen of a 'passive animal world of philistinism . . . thoughtlessly enjoying' its very alienation. Within 'the ingenuous, petty-bourgeois, "home-baked", *common* narrow, horizon of the philistine', as Marx put it, the call to dehumanised man to understand himself as the Marxian alienated labourer, and to transcend his alienation, was either rejected or ignored.

The philistine is often the parvenu—whom romantic critics, themselves often men of somewhat uncertain social standing, fiercely attacked. J. G. Hamann declared that his life's work was 'to show the philistines their nakedness, to unclothe and transfigure them'. The untransfigured many were better educated than their fathers, of course; but Hamann dismissed them as adepts of mere French 'good taste', or abstract men, who received from absolutist society a superficial, mechanical and uniform culture.

Herder's critique of contemporary culture was even more extensive. Urban society offended Herder as it had offended Rousseau. The cities were, claimed Herder, 'chasms' in which man's vital forces were swallowed up; and theatres, libraries, schools and academies were a mere market place, not for true education but for 'paper culture'.

Real human seriousness was lost and 'pedants, schoolmasters, sextons, the half-educated, apothecaries' were free to 'play the scholar'. Just as Rousseau exalted simple peoples, and powerful feeling, over townsfolk and their refined ratiocination, Herder praised the savage's naïve unity, and favoured 'desire, drive and activity' rather than the 'sickly thought' of the cities' bookish autodidacts.

By the time that Coleridge, more than a decade after Herder's death, condemned the incorrigible philistine many as 'sciolists', disastrous progress had been made in educating, or rather—as romantic critics saw it—half-educating the masses; and they, thus bemused and befuddled, had become domiciled in an alienated world where the one knowingly and they unknowingly suffered. The 'multitude of books and the general diffusion of literature', argued Coleridge, 'the more artificial state of society', the very growth of population, caused the rapid growth of 'sciolism'.

Uniform and widespread education had 'mechanised' language 'as it were into a barrel-organ' of formulas and clichés operable even by 'bunglers who have failed in the lowest mechanic crafts'. Their efforts were seen in popular reading matter; in the contents of circulating libraries (whose value Coleridge compared to that of spitting over a bridge); and in the columns of reviews, magazines and newspapers. And, for Coleridge as for many other romantics, the sum of these philistine readers and writers was the 'public', 'shaped into personal unity by the magic of abstraction'.

But the many were more than the ludicrous inhabitants of the realm of alienation. Certainly the many demonstrated into what wretchedness men could fall; yet the many were nevertheless to be found defending and even expanding the realm of alienation. Romantic critics therefore identified the life of the many as a tyrannical normality which perpetuated man's alienated condition.

Such critics variously interpret the tyrannical agencies of this normality. Coleridge pointed to the reviewers, to that sciolist collectivity which 'sits nominal despot on the throne of criticism'. Herder condemned the French and Prussian sovereigns whose systems made men into cogs in a machine; Marx saw tyranny in the person of the capitalist.

An observation of Mary Shelley's illustrates the tyrant's special function in romantic criticism. 'Tyrant' almost has what Coleridge might call a 'barrel-organ' flavour in Shelley's work, so persistently does he denounce kings, Tory ministers and all the rest. But the tyrant has far more than a simply republican, or partisan, significance. 'The subject he loved best to dwell on', wrote Mary Shelley of her husband, 'was the image of one warring with the Evil Principle, oppressed not only by it, but by all—even the good, who were deluded into considering evil a necessary portion of humanity'.

Here is a text for the romantic concept of the tyranny of normality: an 'Evil Principle', accepted even by 'the good', who battle on its behalf against 'one' struggling precisely to transcend the alienation of the many, and restore them to the fullness and unity of their humanity. Not all romantics would necessarily accept Shelley's particular choices of tyrant; but all could recognise, in his representation of the tyranny of normality, that alienated order against which they wished to set the transcendental realm.

### The transcendental enterprise

Romantics contrast the present, alienated realm with another and higher realm of unity and perfection which transcends estrangement and realises the fullness of humanity; and the secularism of the post-reformation era makes of this perfectionism a new, secular religion. As T. E. Hulme noted, 'You don't believe in a God, so you begin to believe that man is a god. You don't believe in Heaven, so you begin to believe in a heaven on earth.'

The secular heaven on earth is sometimes in the past, or in some form of country life which has disappeared from cities. For contemporary historical and anthropological developments encouraged romantic critics to postulate a primordial golden age, from which urban alienated society had fallen. Thus, in Rousseau's *The New Héloise*, Saint-Preux contrasts the artificiality and falsity of Paris with the primitive nobility of the peasants of the Haute Valais, where health, honesty and generosity abound among true men who despise the city's estranging commercialism. Rousseau's ideas shaped later notions about the 'naïve' Greeks, or Nordic man, or the biblical patriarchs; and they contributed to the picture of primitive communism afforded by the 'splendid men and women' who, according to Engels, lived in the 'natural simplicity' of the Homeric or prehistoric 'gens'.

The golden age remained a descriptive rather than a prescriptive notion. That age men had lost, but could hardly regain—except through a reversal of time which romantics did not envisage. Hence Rousseau's most powerful vision is not the golden age of *The New Héloise* but the utopia of *The Social Contract*. Absolutism had sought, Rousseau observed, to join 'the multitude' in 'a single body', so that the sovereign would be 'formed entirely of the individuals who compose it'. If the sovereign had indeed been so constituted, men would have been both free and united: free because only the sovereign could constrain them—and the sovereign was themselves—united because society was founded on men's unity in the sovereign. But absolute monarchy had failed to do this because, although it had joined men together, it had done so by vesting in absolute monarchy an exclusive sovereignty, alien to all other men, thus denying men their freedom, and reducing them to 'herds of cattle'.

Rousseau hoped, nevertheless, to devise a state in which men should be rehumanised in perfect freedom and unity. A true human order, Rousseau argued, would reject absolutism, which merely enforced collective submission, and thereby distorted humanity. Rather, such an order would create a new kind of collectivism that, by realising the 'general will', in which men's true wills and true selves would reside, would enable all men to overcome estranging divisions and imperfections.

The concept of the general will professes to offer men a totality in which the alienation inseparable from their individuality may be lost. The general will transcends the factionalism and misguided self-seeking of individual wills. Indeed the general will directly opposes the particular will of the individual, because the latter is merely the individual's apparent will, a symptom of alienation, while the former is the individual's real, his transcendental will.

This is totalitarian doctrine. But Rousseau did not

find the emotional or intellectual movement in which his totalitarianism could be expressed. The French revolution seemed likely to create such movements, yet both revolutionary republicanism, and Napoleonic imperialism, dissolved more or less into renewed factionalism; and the development of Rousseau's programme was therefore left to Herder and Marx, whose followers shared out totalitarianism among the partisanships of right and left.

Herder replaced the general will with the notion of ethnicity. He believed that the innumerable independent German states fragmented the essential unity of the German race. These states could offer men only an alienated life, because each of their citizens was separated from the unity of the *Volk*, in which resided his essential self. But if this estranging political system could be destroyed, the one vitalising *Volk* spirit could unify all members of the *Volk* in a transcendental state of 'free concurrence'.

The strength of Herder's scheme was also its inflexibility. It presupposed racial and cultural consciousness and it tried to found the state on fulfilment of racial and cultural aspirations. Wherever such consciousness or aspirations were absent, Herder's doctrine must seem foreign if not repugnant.

Marx's concept of the proletariat suggests an economic particularism almost as narrow, and from time to time as useful, as Herder's ethnic particularism. Yet the insidiousness of Marxism lies in the very vagueness of the concept of the proletariat. The proletariat sometimes seems to stand in a specific relationship to the means of production. But he possesses no other distinguishing mark, and this particular relationship can, it seems, be construed in exceedingly wide economic and social terms.

All, it seems, can be admitted to the communist society, which transcends the labourer's estrangement from his labour. This society unites not merely the hitherto estranged members of the now transcended classes but also mental and physical labour, town and country, male and female, theory and practice, thought and being. 'Communism', declares Marx, 'is the riddle of history answered and knows itself to be this answer'.

Marx was much influenced by Hegel, whose own theories propound not merely political but also philosophical transcendence. Hegel often applies logical categories to historical and social affairs. Thus for example Hegel uses for his own purposes the categories of the 'universal' (that is, of concepts such as 'now') and the 'individual' or 'particular' (for instance, any particulars to which the universal 'now' might ever be applied, such as six o'clock, or twelve o'clock).

The universal with which Hegel chiefly concerns himself is *Geist*, 'mind' or 'spirit'. Empirical and particular men are merely alienated, dehumanised and indeed, so to speak, dispirited. But, as human 'minds' or 'spirits', they are potentially that in which *Geist* will be realised. For the present estranging order of 'culture' manifests spirit 'self-alienated' into the various antitheses traced in Hegel's *Phenomenology of Spirit*; and only through the dialectical movements there elaborated can spirit become 'certain of itself' and rise to the state of 'absolute knowledge', in which spirit knows itself in human spirit, and in which the alienation of empirical and particular individuals' human spirit is transcended in unity with the universal spirit.

That transcendence is a philosophical and, more specifically, an epistemological process. 'The tendency of all man's endeavours', writes Hegel, 'is to understand the world'; and, since the world (including man himself) is that in which universal spirit realises itself, to understand it is to achieve transcendental 'absolute knowledge'. And it is dialectical, that is Hegelian, cognition of the world process which constitutes this 'real and true . . . exaltation above the finite'.

Hegel translates religious into philosophical transcendentalism. His early writings consider God as that at which man should strive, and Jesus as supreme man revealed in the achievement of the divine. Shortly before Hegel's death he still expressed the relationship between universal and individual human spirit in semi-religious terms. 'God', claims *The Philosophy of Spirit*, 'is God only insofar as he knows himself. His self-knowledge is, moreover, both a selfconsciousness in man, and man's knowledge of God—which proceeds to man's self-knowledge *in* God'.

The equation between Hegel's concepts and those of traditional Christianity indicates not only the religious origins of Hegelian transcendentalism but also the need, felt by many besides Hegel, to state, in non-religious terms, aspirations for which no generally credible religious terminology could now be found.

Hamann, for example, attempted to revive religious transcendentalism and condemned philosophical transcendentalists as those 'who know nothing of God and fall in love with Mother Nature like fools'. Hamann proposed that humanity should wait upon God, not with the confidence of contemporary rationalist philosophy, but in Socratic ignorance and in the 'dread' that proved man's 'heterogeneity', his estrangement from and in this world. But though Hamann profoundly influenced younger and later romantics, he could not make his strictly religious transcendentalism acceptable to them.

If, in a secular era, religion lost its credibility or significance, but was not to be converted into the abstract language of philosophy, it could always be translated into the more concrete language of art. Art—either in general, or in some specific form, such as music or literature—would then stand for the transcendental condition.

Once art was seen to offer these possibilities, theories of the transcendent significance of art began to develop. These theories identified a realm of utility inhabited by phenomenal man, and an aesthetic realm outside, above or beyond utility. This aesthetic realm is precisely other than the *quid pro quo* of the alienated many who substitute lifeless materialism and acquisitiveness for true humanity. The present order concerns itself, for example, with sensuality or morality; but art provides a higher satisfaction to the one who understands the estranging narrowness of such things.

Transcendental art is a unity, not a collection of

separate artistic works. Aesthetic understanding cannot be derived from contemplating individual aesthetic objects, because such an exercise could lead no farther than a mere inventory of the realm of alienation. Rather such understanding is the knowledge of transcendental beauty: that is, of a beauty whose perfection and unity cannot belong to any single artistic production, or any series of productions, since each of these would be an isolated fragment of the whole.

Romantic artists' pursuit of what Keats called 'the mighty *abstract idea* of Beauty' begins to proceed upon highly philosophical lines. The 'Ode on a Grecian Urn' is, in a sense, a versification of Kant.

> 'Thou, silent form, dost tease us out of thought
> As doth eternity . . .'

The poet declares to the artefact which teaches transcendental beauty beyond knowledge. The poet's communion with this beauty raises him above the estranging mortal realm of merely breathing passion, and merely sounding music, to a higher sphere in whose perfection he is forever sustained. And Keats' higher sphere of immortal love and unheard melodies represents an attempt to create a secular religion from or within the aesthetic: hence the Grecian urn displays a mysterious priest whose unseen sacrifices are worthy of its piper's unheard melody.

What Keats does not propose (except perhaps by his fondness for claret) is the doctrine, familiar to the opium-eating Coleridge, of releasing the estranged self into an aesthetic world of subjectivity and dream.

Those who held such a doctrine believed that man could escape the estranging constrictions of mere phenomenal existence by abandoning the outward role of object and entering, through drink, drugs or other doors to the subconscious, upon a process of interior aesthetic enquiry. The principle of an art above utility thus provides the basis for an art above reason. 'The world becomes a dream, a dream becomes the world', claimed Novalis for whom, as for later romantics, the kingdom of art is a kingdom of fantasy.

## Problems of genius

The transcendental realm is the work of a transcendental agency, humanly speaking, a genius. The genius represents the higher values, and calls to his aid the deepest powers, natural or historical. Yet simply human powers are insufficient to his task. No merely mechanical talent is enough, because talent is the aptitude of the present order, while genius brings about another and perfect order.

Almost every theory of genius expects a violent end to the realm of alienation. The artists of the *Sturm und Drang* period did not doubt that elemental forces must be employed to achieve even *intellectual* triumphs. Thus J. M. R. Lenz' review of Goethe's *Götz von Berlichingen* urged men to throw off the 'eternal slavery' of their present condition, and to become 'images of God', so that 'our unceasing active energy may not rest, may

45

not cease to . . . rage, before it has created freedom about us, room to act: good God, room to act, even if it be chaos that you have created . . .'

Lenz was not alone in holding that man must seek a divine energy—whatever its morality—because that energy contains the fullness of man's power, and concludes his estrangement and degradation. That doctrine may be, and no doubt has been, interpreted as an amoral summons to political greatness. But in all probability it was at first understood to defend a concept of cerebral genius which bears all the marks of political or military greatness. Such genius thinks, feels and acts with violent energy: he is the conquering hero of the realm of the mind.

The romantic category of genius as hero finds its exemplar in the figure of Don Juan, especially as he appears in Mozart's *Don Giovanni*, which was first performed in 1787. Don Juan is an erotic genius whose indefatigable, eruptive sexuality symbolises those deep forces that genius calls to his aid. Furthermore, the immediate satisfaction of Don Juan's desires represents the unification of thought and being, in an area of human experience which strikingly reveals that efficacy of feeling or passion (as compared to mere ratiocination) taught by romantics from Rousseau onward.

Above all Don Juan introduces a new and transcendental order. For so great a lover unites his partners to himself in a rapture which institutes a higher erotic realm over against the estranging bourgeois sexuality of the present condition. Byron's *Don Juan* exposes both Malthus' cold doctrine of economic abstinence:

> But certes it conducts to lives ascetic
> Or turning marriages into arithmetic . . .

and the lascivious prudery of the matchmakers, those

> zealous matrons
> Who favour *malgré* Malthus, generation—
> Professors of that genial art, and patrons
> Of all the modest part of propagation . . .

as the pillars of an alienated eroticism which Don Juan's passion explodes.

Yet Don Juan is also one focus of those romantic tendencies which continually develop into sadism. Romanticism teaches a transcendental art beyond utility and morality: and, what art may be, life of course can be also. Because romantics prefer greatness to happiness—or at least prefer a happiness beyond common utility or morality to the estranging and deadening happiness of bourgeois normality—they open the way to sinister possibilities.

The irrational romantic assumption that alienation is to be overcome by force sanctifies the use of force by whomever shall apply romantic doctrine to himself. The romantics' enthusiasm for Shakespeare's Richard III—whom they identified as demonic power unbridled—illustrates that romantic desire for the greatness of amoral violence to which the figure of Napoleon added a new legitimacy.

But, despite the murder of the commandant in *Don Giovanni*, Don Juan makes his contribution to sadist doctrine as seducer rather than murderer. Sadism

47

offers a peculiar gratification from an amoral, indeed immoral, and useless act of force. The less moral and the less useful the act the closer it corresponds to a transcendentalism that defies and destroys estranging normality. Now the great romantic symbol of bourgeois normality is woman, who expresses the power of alienating worldly sexuality, and from whom the endless alien routine of procreation and domestication cannot be separated. If therefore sadistic gratification be achieved at woman's expense, the transcendental quality of that gratification is redoubled.

In a sense Don Juan's sexual conquests, especially as recorded in *Don Giovanni*, honour and satisfy their victims; but they remain sadistic because these acts of sexual energy ultimately disgrace and destroy the females they possess. Don Juan thus affirms the concept of male transcendental victory over the evil thing-like multiplicity of women; and that concept theoretically justifies the vulgar and dangerous sadism and diabolism of romantic and modernist literature.

Mozart's Don Juan is punished for his crimes, and in his punishment ceases to represent the genius as hero. There is indeed very little purely heroic genius, for even the most optimistic romantics could scarcely believe that genius would simply and unequivocally triumph over alienation. On the contrary, genius is expected to suffer: at the hands of those many who defend their alienated conditions against the one; or under the burdens either of his own alienated consciousness or of his transcendental task.

The notion of genius as martyr, as one who triumphs

48

precisely through suffering, received powerful support from Hegel's theory of the world-historical individual. Hegel argued that the progress of 'the idea', which constitutes world history, required the agency of certain great individuals affined to the idea who, perhaps even in ignorance of the idea's purposes, furthered those purposes nevertheless. But, though such men have the unique privilege of introducing the higher historical order, they are unhappy, as Hegel showed from the examples of Alexander, Caesar and Napoleon. 'They enjoyed no peaceful pleasures; their entire life was labour and toil; their whole nature their passion only. When their end is achieved they fall off like husks from the kernel.'

The world-historical individual suffers partly because he cannot represent more than one phase of the idea's progress. When each world-historical individual completes his task he is destroyed to make way for the next: and in this sense he is martyred so that the transcendent idea can advance. But the world-historical individual must also suffer and be destroyed because each such individual possesses only the alienated character and consciousness of genius in the interim before the transcendental is finally established, and because he therefore displays human limitations and moral weakness that the idea cannot admit. The idea pays the penalty for the problematical morality of world-historical deeds, and for its agents' human limitations, with the lives of these agents, who are thus martyred in order to preserve the morality of the transcendental.

The romantic artist is another example of the category of genius as martyr. That artist is a man, set apart from society, who properly belongs to the transcendental order. He suffers society's reproaches because the philistine many are dedicated to their own alienation which, as Marx puts it, they thoughtlessly enjoy. The artist also suffers society's temptations, because his alienated consciousness, too, contains that estranging element, predominant in the many, which pulls men towards the present deadening normality. Furthermore, the romantic artist's very task, the single-handed introduction of an entire new order, would tax genius' powers even if the world were not hostile to genius and to art. Thus the long line of romantic martyrs, concretely exemplified in the moribund precocity of Chatterton, Novalis or Keats.

Gothic melancholy assists romantics to portray the artist, not crowned in triumphant laurels, but clad in funereal ivy. Goethe's play *Torquato Tasso* treats of the artist's struggle with, and rejection by and of, the world by recounting the poet Tasso's unsuccessful challenge to Antonio Montecatini, secretary of state to the Duke of Ferrara. Though the Duke admires the poet, he supports the reasonable, worldly Montecatini, and inflicts ritual banishment upon Tasso. The poet declares that he has been left

> Forlorn upon a dark and narrow path.
> That horrid and mysterious bird,
> The doleful messenger of darkest night,
> Now presses round and swoops about my head.

Whither, whither must I turn my step
To flee the horror that surrounds me,
And escape the chasm that before me lies?

Here the complex figure of Tasso exemplifies the
romantic idea of the artist: doomed because an artist,
if triumphant in his doom, and the deeper doomed the
greater his art.

Yet Werther is perhaps the best early instance of
the romantic category of the martyr. *The Sorrows of
Young Werther* defines the world as a puppet-show of
tiny men estranged from true humanity. A bureaucratic bourgeoisie has destroyed spontaneous human
life in a mechanical system that tries to regulate even
the passions by administrative rules. Narrow pedantic
philistinism appears in the clergyman's wife who, to
Werther's dismay, interrupts her moral and critical
revision of Christianity to direct the felling of two
mighty walnut trees that inconvenience her dreary
studies. What remains of man in this world of rigid
and petty desolation is the folly of a flower-gathering
lunatic.

Werther identifies himself as the one to overturn the
alienating regime of the many. He studies the heroes
of Homer and Ossian. He aims, though with uncertain
success, to emulate the feats of great men. He com-
pares his sufferings to those of Christ on the cross. His
is a secular Christianity, symbolised in his burial without a priest in unconsecrated ground; and as a secular
martyr his ambitions exceed his achievements. But
Werther remains the romantic Christ, whose sorrows

recall the man of sorrows, and whose defeat presages a sort of salvation.

Werther makes many attempts at such salvation. He first seeks—in painting—an art to mirror the truth of his soul as his soul mirrors the divine. He then hopes that he has found, in the village of Wahlheim, the pastoral simplicity of a naïve golden age preserved into modern times. Finally he discovers, in his love for Lotte, intimations of a humanity which supersedes the shortcomings of the realm of alienation.

But the powers of this realm, within and without, force Werther to abandon painting for mere mechanical production of silhouettes. Conflict and disaster destroy the ideal that he found in Wahlheim. Above all, Lotte's engagement and marriage to another flaunt bourgeois normality before him who had hoped for transcendental love.

Werther must suffer, but his sufferings are true martyrdom. He identifies Lotte as his transcendental 'heaven': 'She is holy to me', he declares. At length Werther shoots himself because he believes that death will release him into a higher world where, before the infinite God, he will eternally embrace his beloved. The novel gives ground to doubt the validity of this belief. Yet though Werther may not be the one, nor his idea of love the transcendental realm, that there can be the one, and that there must be the transcendental, is left in no doubt. And above all, as was demonstrated by the cult of suicide which it evoked, the novel suggests the efficacy of death as martyrdom in a transcendental cause.

That the call to genius is a call to suicide expresses the romantic machochism which forms the reverse to sadism. Romanticism teaches that the transcendental irresistibly appeals to the finest of men, who must, however, suffer in the service of the transcendental. Gothic, and especially English gothic, again makes its contribution, particularly through M. G. Lewis's novel *The Monk*.

Lewis's hero Ambrosio, a genius much more evident than Werther, is destroyed by Matilda, a temptress who represents not the lower demonism of the philistine world but the higher demonism of the realm to which, for instance, Don Juan reaches out. 'Shake off the prejudice of vulgar souls'; Matilda adjures Ambrosio, 'abandon a God who has abandoned you, and raise your self to the level of superior beings!'

The catastrophe devised by Lewis is crude though highly influential. Keats employs similar notions in his own thoroughly, even coldly, considered statement of the myth of an imperative martyrdom of art:

> I saw pale kings and princes too,
>     Pale warriors, death-pale were they all;
> They cried—'La Belle Dame sans Merci
>     Hath thee in thrall!'

Woman's elevation from the mundane evil of objectified and estranging normality to the higher evil of a transcendental realm, in whose amorality the one must suffer even though he may delight, is a felicitous conceit with which to present the ideology of genius. 'La Belle Dame sans Merci' has many daughters, therefore,

down through the inventions of Flaubert and Swin-
burne to Yeats' head-severing queens. Along this route,
as well as by way of de Sade, romanticism descends
into pornography.

Romantics would not agree. Whatever they did was
of the highest and the best and, it seems, for the few.
The idea of genius does suggest a universal achieved
for 'man', and might be assumed to involve a good in
which all men may share. But most romantics summon
up 'man' to reveal the greatness, not the extensiveness,
of the transcendental.

Hegel's transcendental epistemologist, for example,
is one man or perhaps a few. Schiller held that only
finely attuned souls sought his transcendental aesthetic
realm; and he expected only 'a few chosen circles' to
reach that realm. For romanticism derives its dynamic
from the inescapable deficiency of the many who fall
short of the ideal; and the romantics' hostility to the
many is powerful enough to raise the possibility that
the transcendental realm is, to say the least, less than
global.

The romantics suffered greatly from the world which
persecuted them; and their experiences in the world
reinforced their desire to protect their principles from
the depredations of the resilient many. Indeed the
many were particularly successful in acquiring romantic doctrine and converting it to their own ends, meaningless, self-defeating and disastrous as these ends were,
according to the ideology of genius.

While romanticism bent itself to produce transcendental personality—true genius, true martyrs if need

be—philistine popularisation created many spurious little geniuses and spurious little martyrs. 'Every giant ... spawns a dwarf,' observed Marx, 'every genius a leather philistine.' No device could more successfully frustrate romanticism than could debasement of genius, whose relationship to the philistine was, Coleridge observed, that of 'an egg and an eggshell'.

Philistine imitation of genius caused the romantics' resort to esotericism. Hamann, who was perhaps the most thorough romantic exponent of esotericism, presented his doctrines in a series of brief anonymous pamphlets and essays marked by great density of thought, deliberate and sustained obscurity of style and argument, and the most remote illustrations and allusions. Reviewing a quarter of a century of his work, Hamann confessed, 'In some cases I can no longer understand it myself.'

Shelley proved an adept at esotericism. Of his *Prometheus Unbound* Mary Shelley remarked, 'It requires a mind as subtle and penetrating as his own to understand the mystic meanings scattered throughout the poem. They elude the ordinary reader by their abstraction and delicacy of distinction.' Romantics had to keep the ordinary reader at bay, yet this reader's pertinacity proved too much even for the romantics' remarkable talents. The endless problem of philistinism therefore obsessed most romantics, but proved particularly important to the work of E. T. A. Hoffmann.

# HOFFMANN'S THEORY OF GENIUS

## *The estranged world and the alienated self*

JESUS' reply to Pilate, 'My kingdom is not of this world', was Hoffmann's favourite scripture text. For these words expressed in Christian terms Hoffmann's vision of himself, or a projection of himself as genius, rescuing self and world, from their present degradation, and for another, and higher, kingdom.

Life's vicissitudes reinforced Hoffmann's hopes and fears. His parents separated when he was two or three years old; and he could not afford to study music as he wished. He trained instead as a lawyer and took unrewarding jobs in Glogau and Plock, two backward and uncongenial country towns. After a short stay in Warsaw, which he much disliked, the French occupation of Poland caused Hoffmann, as a loyal Prussian, to resign his office and go to Berlin, where he lived for some months in considerable difficulties.

The break in his legal career compelled—or freed—him to spend six years in musical, operatic and theatrical work, first at Count Soden's theatre in Bamberg, and then with Josef Seconda's opera troupe in Leipzig and Dresden. Disagreements with Seconda ended this relatively happy period and forced Hoffmann to return to the law. He spent eight years as a government lawyer in Berlin where he died in 1822 at the age of forty-six.

Hoffmann hoped for greatness as a composer, and

expected to endure mere obscurity as a lawyer. 'It is something quite typical of my life', he wrote, 'that I am always obliged to do what is fundamentally opposed to the true deeper principles of my being'. Eventually Hoffmann's musical criticism and his fiction did bring him a considerable reputation: yet this was no substitute for the acclaim which he wished his musical compositions to receive. Private life gave Hoffmann few compensations for these setbacks. Above all, though more or less happily married, he was profoundly affected by an affair with a young singing pupil, Julia Marc, who married and later separated from a 'shopkeeper' called Gröpel.

These experiences strengthened Hoffmann's belief, derived from his romantic predecessors, that the world was in disorder. Against this disorder Hoffmann reaffirmed Rousseau's notion of the golden age. Celionati the magician of Hoffmann's story *Princess Brambilla*, looks back to 'that wonderful era of sublime joy' when man possessed an 'immediate perception of all being' and 'an understanding of the fundamental pattern, the pure harmony' of existence. This primordial condition of knowledge, harmony and joy has of course disappeared, and Hoffmann often debates man's calamitous transition to modern times.*

* Hoffmann's two novels are available in English translations by Ronald Taylor (*The Devil's Elixirs*, London, 1963) and by L. J. Kent and E. C. Knight (*Murr*, Volume II of *Selected Writings of E. T. A. Hoffmann*, Chicago and London, 1969). *Brambilla*, 'Little Zaches' and 'Meister Floh' have been translated by Charles E. Passage in *Three Märchen of E. T. A. Hoffmann*, Columbia, South Carolina, 1971. 'Don Juan' and other stories are

Thus when Medardus, the hero of Hoffmann's novel *The Devil's Elixirs*, loses his way in a forest he meets a gamekeeper who expatiates upon the difference between unalienated natural man and the alienated inhabitants of the city. The gamekeeper, Medardus realises, preserves 'something of that glorious old freedom' known to man when he 'lived with undivided nature in love and friendship'. Urban man, on the other hand, torments himself in 'walled prisons', where he subsists 'quite estranged from all the splendid things which God has created' for his enjoyment. Because the gamckccpcr is natural man he lives with his hunting companions 'as one family'. But urban man is separated from his fellow men, and even his affinities with natural forces reveal themselves only in momentary happenings attributed to 'chance'.

The Hegelian physician at the court of Prince Alexander of W. tells Medardus more about the estranged world. The physician believes that social relationships, and especially those between nobles and bourgeois, have been dissolved through the historical development of *Geist*. The age of chivalry, argues the doctor, manifested a stable and functional social structure which identified authority with the nobility, to whose personal valour society owed its security.

Hereditary aristocracy successfully bred strength and courage, and efficiently trained the fitness and

included in Christopher Lazare (ed.), *Tales of Hoffmann*, New York and London, 1959. Unfortunately the 'Kreisleriana' have not yet appeared in English translation.

morale of its members. Because war was still little more than personal combat, noblemen could protect society with these qualities alone. 'The scholar glories in his scholarship, the artist in his art, the craftsman and the merchant in their trades. But the knight says, "Suppose a savage foe appears whom you, unversed in war, are unable to defeat. I, the man-at-arms, stand with my battle sword before you: and what is my sport, my joy, saves your lives, your goods and possessions."'

The development of *Geist* replaces physical force by mental process and action by reflection. Above all, the physician observes, spirit has invaded war where organisation and planning succeed to the aristocrat's courage, strong arm and stout sword. Aristocracy has lost its purpose, and become merely quaint or overbearing.

Hoffmann does not care for these changes; nor does he favour the product of progress and enlightenment, namely, the modern rationalist bureaucratic state. Moreover Hoffmann never doubts the enlightened state's tendency to destroy magic, mystery, infinity even, in favour of a prosaic and mediocre materialism. His story 'Little Zaches, known as Zinnober', tells how Prince Paphnutius enlightens his realm by appointing his valet Andres as prime minister. Andres, whose greatest contribution to the Prince's welfare theretofore had been a timely loan of six ducats, has a clear idea of enlightenment. 'We fell the forests,' he explains, 'make the river navigable, grow potatoes, improve the village schools, plant acacias and poplars, make the children sing two-part hymns morning and evening, build roads, and administer vaccinations.'

While government by valet proceeds with this melioristic mishmash, enlightenment science seeks to transform life's mysteries into rationalist truths. Professor Mosch Terpin, a great ornament of Prince Paphnutius' land, explains 'rain, thunder, lightning, why the sun shines by day and the moon by night, how and why the grass grows, etc.' Such activities are intrinsically immoral: Terpin's 'so-called experiments' seem to the hero of Hoffmann's story to be 'a disgusting mockery of the divine being whose breath—in nature—breathes upon us, and arouses in our heart of hearts, the deepest, the holiest sentiments.'

Yet science is more dangerous even than this. For science, Hoffmann believes, destroys man as well as his world. Another of Hoffmann's academics—Professor Aloysius Walter, who appears in 'The Jesuit Church in G.'—is a materialist who teaches that men are machines, whose alleged creative power is really a stomach condition, and whose supposed 'thought' is effected by a junction of brain fibres.

Modern medicine applies these doctrines to maintain and repair patients who have ceased to be men. In Hoffmann's novel *Murr the Cat* Princess Hedwiga exclaims, 'This doctor thinks he can manipulate human nature like a clock which one must wind and dust. How he disturbs me! His drops and essences horrify me. Must my health depend on such things? Then life here below must be a hideous joke of the world spirit.'

Life is just such a hideous joke, in Hoffmann's view,

because science, however disgusting, does tell us what we really are. While in Bamberg, Hoffmann was friendly with the psychiatrist Adalbert Marcus and visited the town's lunatic asylum. What he saw there convinced him that, even if the concept of personality did not entirely misinterpret the human machine, attributes of personality, such as unity and integrity, could not be found in reality, because real men—the allegedly sane no less than the palpably mad—were alienated from themselves. Mesmer's hypnotic experiments, knowledge about which was broadcast by men such as Hoffmann's friend and admirer, D.-F. Koreff, made Hoffmann's point. Hypnosis, Hoffmann believed, proved the existence of a lower mechanical self, separate and distinct from higher consciousness; and mesmerist demonstrations showed that this lower self, given the right stimuli, would perform any tranced, mechanical movements that the hypnotist required.

Technology confirmed the evidence of mesmerism. From about 1740 onwards Vaucanson and other inventors began displaying clockwork automata in animal and human form. These machines encouraged not merely sociological but psychological inferences from clockwork. Hoffmann was much impressed by an exhibition of automata which he saw in Dresden in 1813. The lifeless but motile facsimile man taught the same lesson as the hypnotic subject, namely, that much, if not all, of what we ascribe to human personality is the activity of a biological machine.

Hoffmann concluded that personality was but a

collection of fragments, and that man endured a 'strange madness, in which the true self is divided from itself, so that personality itself can no longer hold together.' Hoffmann used the symbol of doubles to represent the personality thus self-alienated. In part, Hoffmannian doubles are higher and lower selves within one alleged personality. In part, however, they are the fatal *Doppelgänger* (whom to meet was death) prominent in medieval legend and romantic art. Hoffmann used both notions of doubles throughout his work to illustrate what he called the 'chronic dualism' of the alienated self in the estranged and estranging modern world.

## *The musical-erotic paradise*

Among Hoffmann's earliest writings is a story, called 'Don Juan', which tells of the narrator's unexpected visit to a performance of *Don Giovanni*; his encounter with the singer who plays Donna Anna; and her sudden and mysterious death immediately after this meeting.

Then follows Hoffmann's critical analysis of Mozart's opera. Love, argues the 'itinerant amateur' who tells the story, destroys and remakes the elements of human existence. Passion transforms conventional bourgeois life—including bourgeois courtship and marriage—and so reveals the means whereby man can rise above the estrangements of ordinary experience.

Don Juan himself believes 'that, even on earth, he might achieve, through love, through the enjoyment of women, the infinite longing which brings us into immediate intercourse with the supernatural, but which now dwells in our breast only as a heavenly promise'. In short, Don Juan teaches a secular religion in which erotic communion with the supernatural transcends man's alienation from higher existence.

The itinerant amateur is a musician whose character suggests Hoffmann's most influential literary creation, the conductor Johannes Kreisler. In *Murr* Kreisler seeks a paradise known to him only in a 'confused and confusing dream'; and when he climbs the Geierstein, he feels his spirit spreading with eagles' wings to soar to a world of love unlimited by time or space.

Kreisler's erotic paradise, the 'world of light', is promised in the dark blue eyes of Julia Benzon. Julia is 'an angel of light . . . able to unlock paradise'—but only in an explicitly figurative sense. *Murr* complains of Kreisler's extravagance; and Kreisler confesses that his doctrine is open to the simplest commonsense objections. Hoffmann uses Julia's dark blue eyes to represent an order that cannot be expressed in material terms.

Julia Benzon is the fictional counterpart of Julia Marc, whom Hoffmann idealised as 'Käthchen'. But 'Käthchen' was, wrote Hoffmann, only a means 'to induce a kind of poetic somnambulism in which I think that I perceive and recognise the essence of romanticism'. Thus, Hoffmann used Käthchen and Julia

Benzon as *symbols* for the transcendental perfection which gives romanticism its vitality.

In traditional Christianity the transcendental realm was purely and only a good. But the romantic transcendental realm is often amoral, for this realm belongs to an ambiguous secular deity whose demonism makes his realm fit only for a humanity great enough to rise to the demonic. The Christian heaven is for man, the romantic heaven is for great men: such is the reactionary ideological function of the concept of the one and the many.

The demonic element of romantic transcendentalism is not merely reactionary however. Despite the romantics' optimism, they understood both that their systems lacked the authority, and even the credibility, of Christianity, and that their opponents were the vigorous and ever-increasing many. That knowledge instilled in romantics a pessimism which their demonic transcendentalism served also to express.

Because Hoffmann sought to represent the demonic transcendental in sexual symbolism, he tried to find a type of amoral, or immoral, sexuality thoroughly detached from bourgeois normality. Hence his use of the idea of incest which, about 1800, came to represent the higher eroticism pursued, about 1900, for example, in the concept of homosexuality.

Hoffmann seems to have learned the symbolic value of incest from Lewis's *The Monk*, and also from Schiller's *The Bride of Messina*. The chief theme of *The Devil's Elixirs* is the incestuous love between Medardus and Aurelia, which parallels Ambrosio's incestuous passion for Antonia in Lewis's novel. Medardus' and Aurelia's union is condemned—because they are the last members of a criminous and diabolical family whose end God requires: yet no other objection is advanced against these siblings' intercourse. In fact Hoffmann skilfully avoids such objections by emphasising instead the immorality of Medardus' breach of his religious vows of chastity.

The sanctification of Aurelia, who takes the veil, and is mysteriously akin to saint Rosalia, reaffirms Hoffmann's desire to reveal, through the symbol of incest, a state higher than mere bourgeois sexuality, with its rigid social conventions and its unending passion for procreation. This state must be demonic for, though Hoffmann shuns commonplace objections to incest, it is precisely these objections that give incest its power to evoke the horror which elevates sexuality to a higher plane.

But art, in the widest sense, is at least as important as the erotic for Hoffmann's idea of the transcendental. Hoffmann's story 'The Golden Pot' describes art as a utopian 'life in poetry' to which ordinary human existence is blind; and in *The Devil's Elixirs*, Francesco the painter refuses a throne for art because he hopes to recreate the divine spirit, revealed to aesthetic intuition, but concealed in the everyday world of action.

These aspirations assume the highest views of art, and demand the highest type of art—an art which is all art and beyond art. Hoffmann finds music to be the only art that can be so described; and he initiates many of the notions summarised by Pater's dictum that '*All art constantly aspires towards the condition of music*'.

Hoffmann understands music as a universal art, a concept which can be expressed by synaesthesia, the idea of the identity of different sense experiences. Shelley appeals to synaesthesia when he writes,

> And the hyacinth purple, and white and blue,
> Which flung from its bells a sweet peal anew
> Of music so delicate, soft, and intense,
> It was felt like an odour within the sense.

Hoffmann adopts the device in the first series of the 'Kreisleriana'. When Kreisler plays Bach in 'The Musical Sorrows of the Conductor Johannes Kreisler', for example, he feels electric fire in his fingertips and a heavy scent fills the room.

The purest and highest music is instrumental music. 'It is the most romantic of all arts, one might almost say the only true romantic art,' writes Hoffmann, 'because the infinite alone is its subject.' Unlike painting or sculpture, he claimed, instrumental music did not draw its models from the estranged phenomenal world. Unlike opera, instrumental music did not use the human voice with all its references to man's alienated condition. Instrumental music arises from 'the spirit world', and 'opens an unknown realm to man, a world which has nothing in common with the external world of the senses that surrounds him, a world in which he abandons all determinate feelings in order to surrender to an inexpressible longing.'

Yet even instrumental music displays a material substantiality which makes it less than unheard music, the art above all arts—to which, however, music alone can direct us. Hoffmann's story 'Ritter Gluck' introduces a mysterious musician who has entered the spirit-filled kingdom of dreams from which emanates not merely music but, in and through, yet above and beyond, music, a transcendental 'euphony'. Euphony is the Keatsian unheard melody, the true art of infinity, which music prefigures, and which the mysterious musician reveals by conducting an imaginary orchestra and playing Gluck from blank sheets of paper.

The account of 'Kreisler's Musical-Poetical Club' elaborates the concept of euphony. Damage to a piano prevents Kreisler's recital. Instead he strikes a succession of chords on what strings remain, and speaks of the unheard music that accompanies each chord, from 'Chord of A-flat minor (*mezzo forte*)'—'Ah! you bear me away to the realm of eternal longing'—to the appearance of the devil at 'Chords of C-minor (*fortissimo* repeatedly without interruption).'

Like the idea of Käthchen, unheard music reveals the 'essence of romanticism'. Indeed unheard music—universal art—unites with romantic love, which is the universal erotic. Hoffmann portrays the musical-erotic paradise of unified love and art in a series of singer-lovers, inspired by his affair with Julia Marc. As Hoffmann's pupil and beloved, Julia Marc was simultaneously the bearer of Hoffmann's love, and the singer of Hoffmann's songs. Hoffmann represented this transcendental unity in the singer who acts the part of 'Donna Anna' in 'Don Juan', Amalia in 'The Musical Sorrows', and Julia in *Murr*.

'Donna Anna' has sung the itinerant amateur's work. She asks him, 'in the role of – – – in your last opera did you not bring forth from your inner being the enchanted madness of eternally yearning love? I have known you: your soul has opened to me in song! Yes . . . I have sung you, just as your melodies are myself.' Julia's vision in *Murr* repeats this extravagant creed. Julia dreams that she is a radiant melody floating through a splendid garden. She fears that she must vanish with the song. But at once she hears Kreisler declare, 'No! music is not annihilation but ecstasy. I hold you fast with powerful arms, and my song, as eternal as desire, rests in your being.'

Such proclamations, which no doubt owe something to Hoffmann's operatic work, tax the resources of modern sensibility. Yet their romantic grandeur is the product of a calculating symbolism. Hoffmann aims to express the inexpressible, to reveal, even while the condition of alienation remains, at least some idea of the transcendental. Both music and eroticism, which Hoffmann attempted to unite, seemed to offer insights into this idea. What results is 'extravagance', but an extravagance no greater than that of any description of paradise.

This paradise is a demonic and not a traditional Christian paradise, as the symbol of incest indicates. The mysterious musician of 'Ritter Gluck' is not merely delighted but tormented in the kingdom of dreams, where monsters carry him up into the skies or drag him down into the deeps. Hoffmann's essay on 'Beethoven's Instrumental Music' describes the spirit world as a monstrous realm where gigantic shadows destroy all but man's longing for the infinite. Kreisler, the mad musician, is a man elevated yet tortured by his art. René Cardillac, the goldsmith of 'Mademoiselle de Scudéry', soars to the highest heights of art, but is driven by his evil star to madness and murder in the cause of art.

Just as Hoffmann's female singer-lovers express the unity of the musical-erotic, the moral problematic of his demonic paradise is developed in the romantic symbol of the fatal woman who represents masochistic suffering in the service of art. For Hoffmann, art approaches to the transcendental, and partakes of that realm's equivocal morality. The fatal woman therefore displays, not only the ambiguity of aesthetic pleasure, but also the amorality of the higher order which the aesthetic reveals. In Lewis's *The Monk*, Matilda is a devil-woman of great beauty, ability and willpower, who summon Ambrosio to the higher realm, where he is indeed destroyed. Giulietta, in Hoffmann's 'A New Year's Eve Adventure', is a heavenly beauty— but fiend from hell—to whom Erasmus Spikher, in search of the higher life, gives his reflection.

*The Devil's Elixirs* introduces three fatal women: the devil in female form with whom Francesco the painter cohabits, and from whom he draws his inspiration; Euphemia who calls Medardus to the higher realm, just as Lewis's Matilda calls Ambrosio; and Aurelia, for whom Medardus commits his crimes, and in the satisfaction of whose love he would find damnation. Conventional morality, as inherited from the Christian tradition, evidently cannot do justice to the moral possibilities of the transcendental.


## Genius and philistines

Because genius is a secular messiah, he can be understood, especially in the aftermath of absolutism, as a ruler of men. For absolute monarchy establishes the principle that the higher realm is a political realm; and romanticism, though partly a reaction against absolutism, retains something of the political in its interpretation of genius. Thus Hoffmann's Don Juan was 'destined to conquer, to rule' over 'the common herd, over the commodities tossed from the workshop like cyphers before which a digit must stand before they have any value.'

Genius derives its power to rule, to redeem and to create, from an inner kinship with the transcendental. The very smell of the diabolical liquor of *The Devil's Elixirs* dazes Brother Cyrillus, a mere pious Christian, but reinvigorates the ailing Medardus. 'What', Medardus asks himself, 'if the fact that the same aroma which stupefied the feeble Cyrillus—yet did you nothing but good—revealed a secret affinity between your spirit and the forces of nature sealed in that wine?' And of course since God wills Medardus should destroy his own family, and since, by sampling the elixir, Medardus is confirmed upon this criminous course, there *is* a secret affinity between Medardus, that demonic power, and the deity.

Genius's victory is to attain a unity of which Hoffmann often speaks as 'harmony'. Beethoven's instrumental music, for instance, achieves 'a full-voiced harmony of all the passions'. The state of 'poetry' is described in similar fashion. 'After all,' 'The Golden Pot' concludes, 'is Anselmus' bliss anything other than the life in poetry which reveals the sacred harmony of all being as nature's deepest secret.'

When Medardus reaches Rome he explains these transcendental aspirations to the pope. 'Certainly it is a great thing to be a king and rule over a people', observes Medardus. To the man so exalted in life 'all things appear in greater proximity, in greater harmony in every relationship; and from his very eminence arises the wonderful power of surveillance that reveals itself in the born prince as the mark of his higher order.' What can be said of a king can the more justly be said of the pope, who receives 'divine consecration' as 'the regent of the Lord', and whose kingdom, though it embraces all earthly realms, is precisely not of this world.

But until the transcendental work is done, unity evades the one just as it evades the many. Genius himself is divided. Medardus, for instance, is part man yet part devil, whose self-alienation is revealed in the demonic, ghostly double who is his half-brother Count Victor. Thus Medardus' apparent murder of Victor begins, and Victor's real murder of Aurelia ends, the career of transcendental crime of the alienated genius Medardus-Victor.

Genius is alienated because the universal division between one and many is repeated within his own individuality. For the genius' higher self is the part of him which is truly of the one, while his lower self is the part of him which is really still of the philistine many. Giglio Fava, the chief character of *Princess Brambilla*, provides an example. Giglio is a tragic actor whose stupidity and love of money, whose life as the paltry 'stage hero' of execrable melodramas, all define him as a philistine; and his surname (which may be rendered either 'Presumption' or, more prosaically, 'Bean') confirms the point. Furthermore, Jacques Callot, the seventeenth-century artist whose engravings of the *Commedia dell'Arte* Hoffmann adapted as illustrations for *Princess Brambilla*, intervenes in the story to condemn Giglio as a philistine 'boor'.

Yet Giglio's task and achievement is to throw off the estranging philistine order and to rediscover the self, not in the false art represented by the tragedies in which he acts, but in the true art of the *Commedia*. Hence Giglio is divided within himself: the last tragic role he plans to play is the suitably paradoxical part of *The White Moor*. He has within him 'a criss-cross prince', or rather two princes, the philistine prince Taer—the hero of Carlo Gozzi's play *The Blue Monster* —and the royal genius-prince Cornelio; and Giglio's work as genius is to renounce Taer and become Cornelio.

Giglio's alienated personality illustrates a concept

of genius which Hoffmann develops, at greater length, and through even more elaborate use of doubles, in his writings about Kreisler. In *Murr* Kreisler's most evident double is the mad painter Leonhard Ettlinger. Ettlinger, who appears to Kreisler as his dark reflection in the lake at Sieghartshof, evidently represents the philistine imitation of genius. But so does the cat Murr, who is also Kreisler's double. The full title of Hoffmann's novel—*The Life and Opinions of Murr the Cat with the Fragmentary Biography of the Conductor Johannes Kreisler on Random Sheets of Wastepaper*—indicates the conventions upon which it is organised. Murr, the self-educated cat, is the irreducible rationalist philistine, who writes his worthless thoughts on the back of what he has not destroyed or eaten of Kreisler's lofty biography.

*Murr* alternates between Murr's caterwauling and Kreisler's transcendental strivings, which run more or less in parallel. The novel itself is a double, whose structure symbolises both the inner alienation of personality, and the outer alienation of the world into the one genius and the many cats. Indeed the very structure of the novel shows how the many not merely imitate but annihilate the one, in that Murr has consumed or demolished much of Kreisler's life.

Hoffmann's sympathy towards Murr, whose character he claimed to have drawn from his own cat, must not conceal the demonic role assigned to Murr as philistine. Murr's miraculous—or sinister—survival of ordeal by fire and by water hints at a lower philistine demonism in conflict with the higher demonism of genius. Murr's counterpart in 'The Golden Pot' is the evil cat that empowers the witch Liese to tear Anselmus from his search for the higher realm and to affix him to her philistine protegée Veronica Paulmann. Liese reappears, without her cat, in *The Devil's Elixirs*, where she identifies herself with the worldly order by demanding of Medardus a bribe, just as, and immediately after, a venal magistrate requires Medardus to pay for his freedom.

The lower demonism (a demonism which of course justifies the amoral higher demonism of genius) is seen not only in beasts and witches. The philistine Zaches, grotesque child of yet another Liese, gains political power through the demonic forces released by enlightened rationalist absolutism. Zaches' deformity suggests the ugliness of the hideous Italian, who is murdered by Erasmus Spikher in 'A New Year's Eve Adventure', and who points in turn to another motif in Hoffmann's presentation of the conflict between higher and lower demonisms.

Most German romantics looked to Italy for the culture of antiquity and renaissance, and the south's warmth and fullness of life. Goethe's sojourn in Italy realised an ideal that Hoffmann, who never got farther south than Bamberg, desired but failed to achieve. Italy is in part a fairly commonplace romantic good. But Hoffmann the musician also identified the land of Rossini as the source of a trivial and stylish tunefulness which stood in philistine contrast to great German music.

Hoffmann therefore uses Italy to display the seductions of a demonic lower order with which genius must struggle. Thus not merely Spikher, but Berthold, and councillor Krespel in the story of that name, fight Italians, just as Balthasar, the hero of 'Little Zaches', fights Zaches. Medardus is saved by the Italian Pietro Belcampo, who helps him to get to Rome: but that this is an ironic salvation is demonstrated by Medardus' sufferings in Rome where, for instance, his arm is burnt to the bone by a powerful acid. In *Murr*, Kreisler's great rival for Julia's love is the Italian prince Hector—variously condemned as a devil, a dragon, and a basilisk—whom Kreisler ultimately puts to flight.

The conflict between higher and lower demonism is not merely a gothic tournament of fantastic monsters. Hoffmann finds his warring demonisms most of all in everyday life, because it is exactly there that the conflict of genius and philistine arises. For commonplace materialism and hedonism are items in the outward, diurnal phenomenology of the demonic philistinism that condemns humanity to the status of cyphers without an evaluative digit.

'The Golden Pot' portrays the citizens of Dresden as men whose highest aim is to drink beer, and chase girls, in the gardens of the Linke Baths, even though such an existence is as restrictive as the embottled imprisonment wished by the witch Liese upon her philistine prey. So too 'Ritter Gluck' shows how Berliners deafen themselves to transcendental euphony as they hurry off to the zoo.

A number of Hoffmann's works criticise the politics

of the philistine world as a blindness, delusion and feebleness that may imitate but can never achieve greatness. *The Devil's Elixirs* recounts how prince Alexander of W., a caricature perhaps of the grand duke of Saxe-Weimar, allows bourgeois commerce to flourish but so fears the mercantile philistines that he dare not raise from them the taxes needed to make a proper park or run a respectable theatre. While Medardus, the true genius, is caught up in a vast supernatural battle between Satan and a sinister romantic God, prince Alexander thinks he perceives fate in the childish game faro, whose very name recalls the great emperors of an Egypt conquered and rendered impotent in the modern philistine world.

But Hoffmann says more about philistine religion than about philistine politics. Protestantism's secular and democratic tendencies are duly condemned. 'The Golden Pot' contrasts the 'vile unchristian' name (as the bourgeois think it) of Serpentina, who represents the higher love, with the most Christianly named Veronica Paulmann, whose vulgar lust for a title, a smart town house, and all the snobbish joys of the social round, epitomise a Protestant religion whose idea of paradise is the beer gardens of the Linke Baths.

*The Devil's Elixirs* dismisses Protestant clergymen as mere domestics who, having tickled their employers' consciences, are allowed to tuck into the roast. Similar habits are also attributed to Catholics, as represented above all by the gormandising Pater Hilarius of *Murr*. Hilarius and his fellow Benedictines at Kanzheim, the Jesuits at G., and the Capuchins of *The Devil's Elixirs* devote themselves to worldly good cheer rather than the higher things of the spirit. Like Protestants, Hoffmann's Catholic monks are hypocrites, whose affected gait and cant phrases he delights to mock.

Catholicism tends, according to Hoffmann, to a mere vulgar materialism, however much concealed by sentimental piety. Prior Leonardus of *The Devil's Elixirs* is a friend of the philistine Belcampo, and has learned his monasticism in Italy, where he was mistaught that the religious vocation means peace with the world. Such monastic worldly peace is a soothing melancholy that perhaps disguises but nevertheless perpetuates the alienated order.

Catholicism becomes the more dangerous when it attempts a philistine copy of the transcendental enterprise. In *The Devil's Elixirs* the Capuchin Cyrillus claims that the church strives both to grasp the mysterious threads which link this world with the supernatural realm, and to reveal that existence is grounded in a higher spiritual principle. This programme parallels romantic transcendentalism, but the church abjures romantic esoteric doctrine—the doctrine, if only at first, fit for the one alone—for an ignoble philistinism appropriate to the estranged condition of the many. Thus the ignorant faithful are expected to rise to the transcendental by contemplating the rags, bones and bits of wood that pass for relics, or the signs and miracles desired by the superstitious abbot of Kanzheim.

Hoffmann represents the transcendental realm as a musical-erotic paradise. Philistine varieties both of art and of love therefore excite his particular concern. The antithesis of Serpentina and Veronica Paulmann in 'The Golden Pot' illustrates both philistine art and love. Veronica wants Anselmus merely for his person and, above all, his prospects; and to this end she simulates all the ardour of romantic passion. But she reveals her philistine hypocrisy when she loses Anselmus to Serpentina and the higher life, where true romantic passion, and true art, are to be found; for, soon reconciled to her fate, she speedily accepts the suit, and the ear-rings, of the newly promoted councillor Heerbrand, who proposes to her over the soup tureen.

'The Jesuit Church in G.' describes the symptomatic conflict between marriage, the arch-institution of bourgeois normality, and transcendental romantic sexuality. Berthold the painter discovers in the princess Angiola the ideal of beauty which emancipates his artistic powers. But Berthold mistakes this inspiration for the vulgar bourgeois desires embodied in matrimony and, entering into philistine marriage with his ideal, he destroys his wife, his child and himself.

The conclusion to 'The Pause' contains the moral. A composer is inspired by a beautiful singer but, instead of recognising the transcendental in this inspiration, he attempts to 'bring the heavenly down within our miserable worldly limitations. The singer becomes our beloved, our wife perhaps! The magic is destroyed and the inner melody, which once proclaimed the things of glory, is transformed into a complaint over a broken soup dish, or an ink spot on new linen.'

Hoffmann's major critique of philistine sexuality appears in *Murr*. Princess Hedwiga, the novel's Veronica Paulmann, tells Kreisler of Ettlinger's passion for her mother, a passion which drove Ettlinger mad. Kreisler claims that Ettlinger's fate proves him to be no true artist, for when true artists fall in love they 'create great works, and neither die miserably of consumption nor go mad'.

According to Kreisler, there are, on the one hand, true artists, 'real musicians', and, on the other, 'the good people', the many, 'who are bad musicians, or rather no musicians at all'. The real musicians' passion is a spiritual revelation in which they perceive, under the form of the beloved, 'the angelic image' that inspires their art. 'And it is *she*, *she*, the glorious woman, the idea incarnate, who shines forth from the artist's soul, as song—picture—poem!'

But 'the good people' appropriate trivialities of incidental expression in this aesthetic love and use them as the titillating clichés of their own vulgar affairs. 'They shriek "Oh God"—or "Oh heaven!" or, if they are given to astronomy, "oh you stars!" or if they have an inclination to paganism, '"ye gods, she, the most beautiful, is mine, all my yearning hopes are fulfilled"'—and meanwhile they lead off their victim to 'the marriage prison'.

In the same materialist spirit, the philistines reduce art to a mere sexual instrument. In *Murr* the chief experience of art enjoyed by the lecherous baron Alcibiades von Wipp is to seduce the wife of the professor of aesthetics. René Cardillac's wealthy customers hasten to their mistresses' boudoirs with the products of the jeweller's tormented art; and Murr woos Miesmies with his atrocious verses.

Bathos marks these and other exercises of philistine aesthetics. Prince Alexander of W. knows not the depths from which great art springs. He prefers entertainment to scholarship, designs buildings trivial in style and conception and composes tedious and mechanical music. Murr observes that though writing verse is a sweat, poetry does banish earthly sorrow, including hunger and toothache. He plans to publish a volume called *What I Produced in Hours of Inspiration*, including not merely poems such as 'The Desire for the Higher', but side-splitting jokes as well.

The very technique of art is degraded by the philistines. Anselmus' calligraphy, like Werther's silhouettes, is the kind of mechanical 'art' with which the many are most familiar. Berthold's work at the Jesuit church in G. is a paradigm of philistine art, for his job is to paint wood like marble—as if a copy, on an inferior substance, of the measurable surface features of stone, could replace the living rock of divine creation.

### Genius, suffering and martyrdom

Romantic genius is divisible into two categories, that of the hero and that of the martyr. The heroic category, in which genius triumphs outright, over circumstances or foes, can be traced in certain phases of

characters such as Don Juan, and in certain achievements of historical figures such as Beethoven or Napoleon. Yet in most cases romantic genius not merely
suffers but triumphs through his suffering. Hence the
category of the martyr, which dominates romantic
thought, and links romanticism with modernism.

Hoffmann's work contains little of romantic genius
as hero. Few of his characters can be seen as a genius
revealed at his very moment of victory; and Hoffmann
indicates his unease with the heroic category by the
restrictions which he places upon such spectacles. 'The
Golden Pot', which seems to offer such a display, is an
apparently ingenuous story about an ingenuous adoles-
cent. That Anselmus is genius is contestable, and his
ascent to the life in poetry is largely the work of others.
It is Serpentina who reveals to him the possibility of
the higher realm; and it is Archivarius Lindhorst who
defeats Liese the witch and releases Anselmus from
his crystal prison.

Anselmus does pledge himself to the transcendental,
and his steadfastness, Lindhorst declares, overcomes
'the hostile principle that strove to enter your being
and to divide you against yourself.' But as Anselmus
flies to paradise on the fairy wings of fantasy, the
suspicion remains that he is merely a child who goes
where all good children go.

Most of Hoffmann's works recount the woes of a
harder world than that of 'The Golden Pot'. In that
harder world the one suffers at the hands of the many.
The mysterious musician of 'Ritter Gluck' describes
himself as one of the damned, doomed to wander in

the wastes of philistine Berlin where art is as cold as Lapland. Others share his fate. The 'Kreisleriana' begin with 'The Musical Sorrows of the Conductor Johannes Kreisler', in which, at the end of a philistine salon, the musician bitterly announces, 'like the convalescent who cannot stop telling what he suffered, I note here in detail the hellish tortures of today's tea.'

This and subsequent pieces relate how the bourgeois many dismiss transcendental music as an entertaining pastime, and despise musicians as weakheaded menials useful only to train up bourgeois children. Perhaps worst of all the philistines attempt art themselves, opening their mouths to 'shriek, squeak and caterwaul, gargle, groan, moan, quaver and quack' in hideous mockery of 'wonderful, holy *musica*, whose delicate being is so easily desecrated.'

In *Murr* Kreisler recounts his unhappy experiences as conductor at the grand ducal court, where etiquette and ignorance combine to force genius into the constricted role of a cultural functionary. Here, as everywhere else in alienated society, the one is required to surrender his transcendental aspirations and to remain a cog in the machine. 'Let the fine composer become a conductor or musical director', exclaims Kreisler, 'let the poet become court bard, the artist court painter, let the sculptor chisel court likenesses, and you will soon have no more useless visionaries in the land, but instead useful burghers of good education and harmless morality.'

The philistine world invades the personality of genius. Hoffmann wrote of his stay in Bamberg that the world's opposition to 'the higher life, where man raises himself above the stinking bog of miserable starveling existence, caused in me a disharmony, an inner conflict, which had much more chance of destroying me than any external disturbance' of war. Indeed Hoffmann portrays the genius's very self as being at war with itself. Thus, for example, the masked duels of *Princess Brambilla*, in which the cardboard puppet Giglio Fava is destroyed by the transcendental Prince Cornelio Chiapperi, who thus emancipates the true genius Cornelio-Giglio.

Inner disunity must dominate genius until his transcendental work is completed, whether the anguish induced by that domination is merely the misfortune of the suffering hero, or the very task of genius as martyr. The distinction between these two concepts is highly important to romantic notions of genius. For romantics hold that, while Napoleon on campaign, for example, must endure hardships which (though inescapable) are quite incidental to his political and military achievement, a Beethoven must suffer in order to develop from within himself the unique greatness of his art, which can be created in no other way.

That idea is illustrated in *Murr* by Kreisler's flight from the palace of Sieghartshof to the abbey at Kanzheim. At Sieghartshof, in the world, Kreisler's manifest 'dissonance', his estrangement from, yet in, the alienated condition, torments him, yet enables him 'through powerful magic' to conjure up 'mighty spirits'

83

from 'the depths of harmony'. In Kanzheim, spuriously out of the world, Kreisler ceases to know suffering, because a philistine religion has secretly compromised with the alienated order: and here his creative powers so decay that he can only write trivial music of 'a sweet and pleasant sadness'.

Medardus is a much more complex figure than Kreisler. Yet these two martyr-geniuses are closely connected. Kreisler takes refuge in one monastery; Medardus is brought up in another, Kreisler is a musician; and Medardus is at least a musical critic. Furthermore 'Medardus' is a monastic, that is, an assumed name and, it is hinted in *Murr*, 'Kreisler' is an assumed name also.

Kreisler derives his name from *Kreis*, 'circle', and urges that the word 'will make you think of the magic circles, in which our entire being moves, and from which we cannot escape'. 'The circler (*der Kreisler*) circles in these circles', disputing with 'the dark unsearchable power' that described them, but—'wearied by the St Vitus dance which he must perform'—ever longing to be free. Thus the circler-genius suffers the St Vitus dance of man's insane estrangement of which, through the suffering of his dispute with the dark power, he will cure himself and mankind.

Medardus' name, which Hoffmann perhaps found during his psychiatric studies, has the same significance as Kreisler. For the name alludes to the Convulsionaries of St Medard, a Jansenist sect which suffered convulsions and cured them in the cemetery of St Medard's church in Paris. Hoffmann's Medardus is, like

84

Kreisler, the one who, himself alienated and tormented will release the puppet many from the circles in which they dance.

The dark power with which Kreisler disputes may be a lower or, more ambiguously, a higher demonism. The latter interpretation points to a significant element in romanticism. For the transcendental is not merely the greatest height of human achievement but an achievement which demands the utter transformation of alienated man. The transcendental manifests a vastness, even an otherness, which at least appears to threaten all who attempt it: although precisely as the greatest human achievement, the transcendental must have some mysterious affinity even with alienated humanity.

Hence a paradox in the ideology of genius. Romantics often express the affinity between man and the transcendental as unity with the divine; but the divine is as often interpreted as an amoral demonic force outside and above bourgeois normality. And because man, even genius, must perceive this force at least partly as a threat, romantics intimate the suffering so imposed through the symbol of a demonic paradox, in which man must challenge the god he serves.

Genius is in this sense a wrestling Jacob who must strive with God and prevail: Medardus presumptuously claims to be St Anthony; councillor Krespel confesses the desire to become God; Berthold speaks of art as a promethean defiance of the gods. But to our present, imperfect human understanding the demonic paradox means not merely suffering but calamity. The editorial foreword to *The Devil's Elixirs*, for example, concludes that he who presumes 'to challenge the dark power that rules over us' must be 'taken for lost'.

The archetype of wrestling Jacob has much in common with Hegel's concept of the world-historical individual. The world-historical individual forwards the historical progress of the idea, usually unconsciously, through deeds which, though perhaps criminal, are still necessary to introduce successive eras in the development of both the idea and mankind. Medardus does the will of God, usually unconsciously, through deeds which are manifestly criminal, yet latently good, because they are God's will. For Medardus's divinely appointed task is to destroy his own diabolical family, the salvation of mankind from which can only be achieved by immoral acts including murder.

Hegel's idea and Medardus's God are amoral forces to whom, it might be thought, what is usually understood by immorality would be no less acceptable than what is usually understood by morality. But Hegel and Hoffmann wish to preserve at least the symbolism of morality, and both therefore demand penalties from criminal world-historical genius.

In Hegel's theory, the world-historical individual suffers for his deeds and thus keeps the idea unsullied; in *The Devil's Elixirs* Medardus undergoes ineffable punishment to protect the supernatural goodness of God. Because both the world-historical individual's and Medardus's expiation of guilt arises directly and necessarily from that guilt, through which alone they can advance God, man, or idea, both enter the category of genius as martyr.

Medardus exemplifies the fatality of such martyrdom. He must bring his family to an end through an inescapable, divinely ordained self-immolation. He must deny his passion for his half-sister Aurelia, because consummation of this passion will continue the diabolical line; and he and she must die because only when they are dead is the line finally terminated. Medardus's transcendental task, his restoration of God's will in a world estranged by satanic power, depends not only upon criminal acts for which Medardus must be punished, but directly upon his suffering and death, without which that task cannot be completed. Medardus is a paradigm of the martyr as interpreted by the esoteric theology of romanticism.

# 3
## KIERKEGAARD AND
## THE ROMANTIC CRISIS

### *The present age*

KIERKEGAARD inhabited the final epoch of Danish absolutism, the democratisation of which occupied more or less the years of his adult life. By developing urban society, rational social and administrative method, and new techniques of education, absolutism prepared the way for democracy and, in so doing, earned the opposition of romantic critics. But by Kierkegaard's time the threat of democracy had to some extent materialised, and absolute monarchy which, in the right circumstances, might be a useful anti-democratic instrument was, in states such as Denmark, almost too weak to sustain criticism. Thus the realities of the 'present age' demanded a kind of defence of absolutism—which Kierkegaard was indeed anxious to offer—if only on terms of his choosing.

Kierkegaard used the theories of the German romantics and above all Hegel to explain the present age. Such theories interpreted history as a triadic pattern in which man once was united with himself and his world, if united only within the confines of a limited existence; is now divided from himself and his world, even though his existence offers infinite possibilities; and will be re-united with self and world in a future order of infinite, transcendental humanity.

Hegel's quasi-logical version of this pattern treated man's existential situation as a relationship between universal and individual or particular. That universal of which man is the individual is his human *essence*, while his individuality, his particular being, is his *existence*. In the past, individual or particular man was united with the universal. In the present, however, his existence is estranged from the universal; and since the universal contains man's essence, such estranged existence is an inferior, a dehumanised existence.

Hegel describes individual man's lost, past relationship with the universal as an 'immediate' relationship, lacking human self-consciousness. Modern man, who has such self-consciousness, suffers the 'duplication', the alienation, inseparable from his estranging reflectiveness; but future man, precisely because he possesses self-consciousness, will enjoy absolute knowledge through the process of transcendental dialectical cognition.

Such optimism is generally foreign to Kierkegaard. But he does adopt much of Hegel's theory of history. Hegel distinguishes between *the* universal, *das Allgemeine*, so to speak, which he understands as universal *Geist*, 'spirit' or 'mind', which is the 'productive idea' that develops itself in history; and, as it were, *subordinate* universals, the successive 'moments' of the productive idea which appear to men as 'the existent', *das Bestehen*, of any one, phenomenal stage in the idea's development. Similarly Kierkegaard distinguishes between the universal, *det Almene*—which he translates into his concept of God—and the existent, *det Bestaa-ende*, through which the universal appears to men.

For Hegel and for Kierkegaard the existent—the entire human order, social and historical, which we perceive at any one point in time—is, however, no more than a moment of the universal, which continually develops itself by destroying one moment in another. Thus arise the 'collisions', of which both Hegel and Kierkegaard speak, in which, while ordinary human individuals must seek to align themselves with the universal norms mediated to them through the existent, world-historical individuals express their deeper affinity with the universal by breaking these norms in order to replace the old existent with a new.

Kierkegaard treats the present age as an existent, through whose ideal normality the universal shines, and whose ideal norms ordinary human individuals should obey—and would obey, but for the corrupting influences of liberalism, democracy and constitutionalism. Yet as an existent, the present age is but one moment of the universal; and its contemporary corruption (liberalism, democracy and constitutionalism included) merely bedims the universal, which therefore seeks, from a world-historical individual, the radiance of a new existent.

'As a rule', writes Kierkegaard, 'the highest but qualitatively the significant duty which is put to any man', is to be 'the normal, the regular individual', who 'unfolds the life of the existent in his own existence'. The normal individual, rather like the past man of the triadic pattern of history, exists in immediate unity with the universal. He is unalienated man, fully himself, fully subjective, and one with the higher human values of the universal in which his essence resides. He is therefore 'free and essentially independent', even though his existential task is to reproduce and renew 'the life of the existent within himself'.

But Kierkegaard also defines another type of individual, who 'renews' the universal not by reproducing it in his own existence but by providing 'a new starting point' from which the universal can progress to a higher moment of its development. Although Kierkegaard does not use Hegel's term 'world-historical individual', but calls this latter category 'the special individual, the extraordinary', the Kierkegaardian extraordinary stands in the same relation to the universal as the Hegelian world-historical individual stands to the idea. For the world-historical individual forwards the idea even when he appears most hostile to the idea's manifestation in the contemporary existent; and the extraordinary forwards the universal even when his 'new starting point' appears most hostile to the contemporary existent of the universal. Thus the special individual is related to the universal by the paradox that he is both for it and against it.

In the ideal past, men were existentially subjective, unalienated individuals. But, claims Kierkegaard, man becomes reflective and hence alienated; and produces, from objectified self and objectified existent, a 'normality' now merely estranging. Kierkegaard's concept of reflection may owe something to Schiller. Indeed *Either-Or* uses the idea of reflection, much as Schiller might use it, to distinguish 'naïve' Greek drama from modern, 'sentimental'—that is, in the Schillerian sense, reflective—drama.

The tragic hero of classical antiquity, argues Kierkegaard, stood within and was united with the categories of family, state and race. Although tragic, he was therefore unalienated. The tragic hero of modern culture, like modern man, is so abstract that he has reflected himself out of these categories. Unlike the classical tragic hero, or the normal individual, he does not reproduce the existent in himself. He stands isolated and alienated, self-producing, his own creator. Yet, despite this apparent divinity, he is no subjective unity but two estranged selves, a reflecting subject—easily reversible into an object—and an object reflected upon.

The growth of reflection is a process of subversion, as Kierkegaard's view of the history of religion reveals. In the past, probably in the middle ages, he assumes, man was truly human in the immediate, all-embracing seriousness of his devotion to God, with whom he could be united if only through the grace of the Almighty. Then religious man became reflective man. Luther identified salvation with the phenomena of religious faith, and thus turned God into man and man into God. Religion became merely one of life's ingredients: the state of mind which men equated with faith, and to which they attributed divine significance. Such a state was the mood of the 'quiet hours' to which, in Kierkegaard's view, the religion of the present age is addicted.

Yet the 'quiet hours' represent not simply vulgarity but a challenge to God, whose infinity is reduced to a state of man's mind. Godlike powers are thus conferred on an abstract idea of *humanity*, 'the *summa summarum* of all men'. This abstract man, in fact an object of reflection, but in pretence a deity whose very 'quiet hours' were divine, was meant to overawe God, just as in the present democratic age 'the multitude overawes the king, and newspapers overawe councillors.'

For though the distinction between God and man is abolished 'first grandly, in speculation' by 'a chosen circle of philosophers'—that is, the German romantics —it is then re-abolished 'vulgarly, in the highways and byways' by the philistine masses, so that despite the philosophers' devotion to the concept of the one they end by teaching 'that the mob is God incarnate'.

The doctrine that, because the abstract '*summa summarum* of all men' is divine, all men are made equal in their common divinity, spread rapidly. The inventions of the age, above all the printing press, served to distribute both democratic principles and the habits of thought conducive to such principles. Lexicons, summaries and text books purported to provide democratic learning for all, while journalists took the ordinary man's hard earned money in return for lessons in subversion that only made him unhappy. Ultimately enlightenment education and liberal journalism produced the *public*, an abstraction which simultaneously objectified its members as uniform, alienated units and attempted to level to its own depths all the authority that the present age had retained.

The abstract, objectified humanity which composed the public necessarily threatened social order. The

'omnibus' of the Hegelian 'system'—polemically mis-
interpreted by Kierkegaard as the enlightenment's
final achievement—enabled the most plebeian to take
whatever intellectual journeys they chose. Thus trained
in ideas, Kierkegaard believed, people had ceased to
exist in direct, personal relationships with each other,
pupil and teacher, subject and king, for instance; and
had become third parties reflecting upon objective
situations, in which they existed, but from which they
had mentally abstracted themselves. Hence people
were free to debate 'problems', such as 'education' or
'the constitution'—and they found it much easier to
discuss the structure of government than to judge the
merits of a pair of shoes.

The political machinery of the present age realised
these ideas. Kierkegaard identified the development of
political parties with the doctrine (which he attributed
to liberalism) that, however mediocre men might be
as real human individuals, the mere weight of their
abstract numbers made their opinions (when voiced
by an association) at least equal to the considered
judgment of first-class minds.

Constitutionalism, though apparently non-violent,
had a similar revolutionary tendency. 'A passionate
tumultuous age will *overthrow all, invalidate all;*' noted
Kierkegaard, 'a revolutionary but dispassionate and
reflective age transforms this show of strength into
*a dialectical feat, which lets all stand but corruptly cheats it
of meaning.*' Thus liberal constitutionalists proposed to
keep the monarchy but to destroy its authority.
'People will not have the royal power abolished—by

no means—' Kierkegaard wrote, 'but if little by little they could transform it into a figment, then they would shout "Hurrah for the king" with pleasure.'

The many who constitute the subversive public of the present age demonstrate typical philistine devotion to their own alienated condition. Kierkegaard delighted in Hoffmann's picture of a bourgeois mentality, unable to rise above time and space, but capable of reducing all life's existential seriousness to a formula. *Either-Or* mocks the philistine many as people who think that the meaning of life is a good position, and that promotion is the goal of life; that love's dream is an heiress, and that a loan is true friendship. Such men, Kierkegaard concluded, save no more from the great fire of life than the housewife who rescued the tongs when her house was ablaze.

To Kierkegaard the Danish state Lutheran clergy exemplified the philistine character. In the last year of his life Kierkegaard published the series of polemical articles and pamphlets translated into English as *Kierkegaard's Attack upon 'Christendom'*. The *Attack* contrasted the true martyr Christ with the clerics' self-seeking philistine imitation. Jesus was the man of sorrows, humiliated, mocked and spat upon, who suffered death on the cross yet rose from the dead. The self-appointed priests of Christendom, Kierkegaard observed, were actors in fine clothing who, for a fee, played dramatic scenes in beautiful buildings.

But the philistines could not escape what, in *Fear and Trembling*, Kierkegaard called 'the terrors of existence'.

Schiller had claimed that reflective man in the age of reason lived in a condition of 'fear and sorrow', because he was divided between the demands of his animality and a longing for transcendental infinity. Kierkegaard argued that man was a synthesis of finite and infinite, body and soul, and that this synthesis was the work of spirit. During life, the human synthesis is always in a state of mere becoming; and moreover, in the present fallen state of man, this synthesis is outside the control of the divine power that should sustain it, because God's will is constrained by man's sinful freedom. Man experiences the consequent alienation of his being as 'dread' or 'despair'. In existence, Kierkegaard writes, the dagger is not stayed, the wound is open, the worm dieth not, the fire is not quenched.

Kierkegaard tends to associate 'dread' with the naïve state of immediate unity, and 'despair' with the reflective state of modern man. He assumes that the philistine many, as reflective modern men, must always and in every instance despair; and, like Marx, he reckons with their manifest self-satisfaction by treating their despair as unconscious despair.

The form of despair common to 'natural man in Christendom' is 'ignorance of being in despair', argues *The Sickness unto Death*. 'Philistinism is spiritlessness . . .' concludes Kierkegaard; but this dead complacency is of course 'also despair', because it is precisely lack of spirit which alienates being, and hence causes despair. 'The philistine has lost himself and God', therefore, even though his despair may be recognised only by his 'spiritless peace of mind'.

## *The tyranny of normality*

Kierkegaard experienced the present age as a corrupted 'existent', as a 'normality' which negated the universal. Indeed he regarded this normality as a tyranny which intruded into, and threatened to destroy, his own life. This tyranny first revealed itself to Kierkegaard in the person of his father, M. P. Kierkegaard. Much has been made of Kierkegaard's alleged devotion to his father. But M. P. Kierkegaard typified the vulgar bourgeois worldliness that his son condemned.

The elder Kierkegaard started life as a shepherd boy but, when the government began to abolish serfdom, hastened to Copenhagen at the age of twelve. There he made one fortune in trade and another, like the Jews, in speculation during the Danish state bankruptcy in 1813.

Though a mere 'hosier', as his son termed him, M. P. Kierkegaard became a wealthy and eminent citizen, a monument to the Danish crown's liberalisation policies, and a close friend of the head of the Danish state church, J. P. Mynster. Whether Kierkegaard attacked the bourgeoisie, the decay of absolute monarchy, or the spread of social and political power among the poor, his father always furnished an uncited example.

M. P. Kierkegaard brought this alien normality to bear against his son. The father grandly believed himself under the special judgment of God who, he told his son, he had cursed when a boy. Since this curse was followed not by divine retribution but by remarkable worldly success, M. P. Kierkegaard (according to his son) produced an explanation worthy of Hoffmann, to whom Søren Kierkegaard felt, he wrote, 'closely related in many ways'.

The Kierkegaards might seem to enjoy God's blessing; but they were a doomed family, in which the father's guilt would fall on the children, whom he would survive. 'When I saw in my father an ill-fated man who should outlive us all, a cross upon the grave of all his hopes,' wrote Kierkegaard, 'I felt the stillness of death deepen around me. Guilt must rest upon the whole family, God's punishment must be upon it; it would vanish, struck out by God's mighty hand.'

The elder Kierkegaard seemed thus to threaten his son with a demonic philistinism. The son alleged he was taught that, like a sort of Christ, he would die in his thirty-third year, to expiate his father's sins. Some kind of childhood injury intensified this sense of destruction. Kierkegaard represented himself as a man cursed, deformed, and debarred from human happiness, by ancestral sin. His father's melancholy compassion was no comfort. Kierkegaard used his real or imagined hunchback to identify himself with the arch-villain of romanticism, Shakespeare's Richard III, of whom he asked in *Fear and Trembling* 'What made him a demon? Evidently that he could not bear the pity to which he had been subjected from childhood.'

Kierkegaard responded to his father's menaces by abandoning his father's religion. 'I grew up, so to speak, in orthodoxy', wrote Kierkegaard shortly after his twenty-second birthday, 'but as soon as I began to think for myself, by degrees the immense colossus'— an apt description of the elder Kierkegaard—'began to totter.' Kierkegaard made no effort to read for the theology degree which his father wanted him to take, and devoted himself to the German romantics while he awaited fulfilment of the paternal prophecies.

To his surprise, his father died in August 1838. One month later, Kierkegaard published his first book— under the defiant title, *From the Papers of One Still Living*; and in three years he completed both the theology degree and his master of arts thesis, on which he had scarcely begun in the previous eight years of idleness.

Kierkegaard attacked his father, directly or indirectly, in later writings, and especially in *Fear and Trembling* where an equivocal Abraham plans to satisfy his religious beliefs by murdering his son. Above all, apparently in the continued expectation of death at thirty-three, Kierkegaard squandered his father's money with an extravagance that liquidated both the taint of bougeois commercialism and his father's achievements.

Meanwhile Kierkegaard sought a career as publicist and philosopher. He hoped to become the intellectual arbiter of Copenhagen society and, as such, to defend the monarchy against bourgeois liberal constitutionalism. Kierkegaard did not understand the crown's share in promoting its own reform through political, social and economic measures, some of which antedated

Kierkegaard's birth; nor did he realise that the monarchy's occasional forays against the liberals concealed a willingness to compromise with them when the need arose.

In 1845 King Christian VIII clashed with the liberals and the peasants over the right of political assembly and the freedom of the press. Kierkegaard could only approve the king's stand, but was perhaps unaware that the crisis convinced Christian that he should introduce a new constitution. While the king's ministers drafted this document, which was completed shortly before Christian's death in January 1848, Kierkegaard determined to attack the liberals.

He denounced a literary rival and revealed him to be a secret editor of the most notorious Danish liberal paper, *The Corsair*, whose staff the government frequently imprisoned. Kierkegaard also invited the *Corsair*, which opposed his politics but admired his talents, to cease praising him—and instead to satirise him as the paper satirised the dignitaries of Copenhagen. To Kierkegaard's horror, the *Corsair* accepted his invitation, and subjected him to a campaign of mockery which lasted through most of 1846.

Although the government appreciated both Kierkegaard's royalism and his dialectical powers, it hesitated to defend this notorious reactionary in view of the settlement with the liberals for which it hoped. Kierkegaard received from the court and its environs no protection or sympathy whatever during the ordeal of 1846.

The government's inaction was not merely a blow to Kierkegaard's pride. By 1846 the devotion with which he had spent his inheritance threatened him with difficulties only postponed by the sale of his father's house. Kierkegaard needed money and first hoped to get it from the crown which he defended. But in the political circumstances of 1846 the crown could afford to pay Kierkegaard's bills no more than it could afford to punish his enemies. No money was forthcoming.

Kierkegaard now interpreted the *Corsair* episode as a plot against himself and his principles. He believed that he had been allowed to attack the *Corsair* only to be the scapegoat of the established order. 'The aristocrats', he wrote early in 1847, 'will remain cowards and keep quiet in envy, leaving me to go on and then letting me fall in order to profit by it all in the end.' The crown, he feared, was at the head of this subversive conspiracy; and these fears were justified in 1848 when the new king Frederick VII let the liberals into power and accepted a constitution going well beyond that prepared by his predecessor.

The *Corsair* episode shocked Kierkegaard. His father had betrayed him before he was born; his king had betrayed him in the hour of his great self-sacrifice. He would reply with a supreme polemic, not directly against the philistine many, the mere creatures of an alien normality, but against the tyrants themselves.

Because he could not bring himself openly to attack father or king, he chose J. P. Mynster for his target. Mynster was not only the king's representative in

religious matters, but also a close friend of Kierkegaard's father: so close indeed that Kierkegaard confessed of Mynster, 'Whenever I think of him, I shall
always think of my father.'

Mynster was not, Kierkegaard believed, a world-
historical figure like himself, out on 'the 70,000 fathoms'
of destiny. At best the bishop was the normal individual because he had 'always clung fast to the existent,
and is now quite grown into it'. But Kierkegaard soon
thought worse of Mynster. Mynster, he claimed, was a
careerist, a traitor to Christianity, a 'Sunday orator', a
liberal, a journalist, a coward. Such accusations in-
vigorate Kierkegaard's *Attack* upon Mynster's philistine religious system.

But Kierkegaard did not publish this polemic for
nearly eight years after it had first taken shape in his
mind. He drew back, not only because he hesitated to
attack the symbol he had appointed for his father and
his king, but for prudential reasons. When he failed to
get a royal pension, Kierkegaard hoped for a church
appointment, first a city living, later a position in the
pastoral seminary. Mynster refused him both posts;
and for some years Kierkegaard was caught upon the
dilemma that, if he issued his polemic against the
bishop he would not get the job, but that if he got
the job his polemic would be hopelessly compromised.

When Mynster died, in January 1854, circumstances
were not such as to give Kierkegaard's polemic the
character he desired, namely, of an attack not simply
on Mynster, or on Mynster's church, but on the entire
estranging, tyrannical normality for which they stood.

But during 1854 Denmark faced the prospect of a new, and more radical, constitution as soon as the National Liberal and Peasant parties could end their differences and organise a coalition to draft such a document. These two groups allied themselves together in December 1854.

Kierkegaard at once published his first article against Mynster and continued his attack until 2nd October 1855. On that day the new constitution was adopted and Kierkegaard collapsed in the street. Before he died, Kierkegaard took the opportunity to relish his battle with the tyranny of normality. 'You have no idea', he told his friend Emil Boesen, 'what a poisonous plant Mynster was, you have no idea how prodigiously he disseminated his depravity. He was a colossus. It wanted great strength to tear it down, and it was bound to fall on him who did it.'

## Existential genius

The present age displays merely an objectified humanity. Man has become thing: whether that thing be the humble psychological object of scientific enquiry, the lofty abstraction of pantheistic philosophy, or the sovereign 'people' of democratic politics. Existentialism is a proposal to transcend this objectification by restoring man's existential subjectivity. Man must know himself as subject, as 'individual' once more. He must escape his present estranging disunity; he must stand outside the alienating operations of modern culture; and he must address himself with seriousness to the 'tasks of existence'.

The young man of *Repetition* learns this lesson. One can, he believes, 'be in oneself alone', 'living immured within one's personality'. In existential subjectivity, he declares, 'I am myself again. This "self", which another would not pick up in the street, I own once more. The division within my being is transcended, I am again united.'

Transcendental reunification of being means separation from the present estranging normality. In *Fear and Trembling* the 'knight of faith' must shun the resting places of this normality and seek 'a lonesome way strait and steep'. In particular, he who aspires to existential subjectivity must belong not to the humdrum round of family, household and marriage but to the great, semi-Hegelian 'idea' through which, Kierkegaard believes, God speaks. 'I am where my soul's desire was . . .', the young man reports of the transcendental state. 'I belong to the idea. When it beckons I follow, when it appoints an encounter I await it day and night. No one calls me to dinner, no one expects me at supper.'

Kierkegaard's concept of the transcendental indicates his response to the crisis of romanticism. For Hoffmann the transcendental was still a condition to which even the many would gladly aspire if they could, and to that extent Hoffmann remains a romantic. But for Kierkegaard, who is to this extent a modernist, desperate may be the 'terrors of existence' in the alienated realm, the transcendental—even by comparison with those terrors—manifests a forbidding austerity.

Kierkegaard expresses existential subjectivity as something strongly reminiscent of the conventional Christian life of faith. But Kierkegaard's deity is not the mere instrument of human purposes to which conventional Christianity reduces God. Kierkegaard's God is a demonic force, an infinite psychic power, certainly in some sense available to the existentially subjective man of faith, but at the highest of prices.

*The Sickness unto Death* explains that in Christianity 'every individual man' is 'invited to live with God on the most intimate footing', but concludes, 'if anything would make one lose one's reason, surely it is this!' 'Humanly speaking', we learn from *Fear and Trembling*, the knight of faith 'is mad'; and his madness is a good deal gloomier and more destructive than the sublime insanity of Hoffmann's concept of the transcendental.

Greatness is needed to introduce existential subjectivity, therefore; and Kierkegaard expects this greatness to be embodied in the one, the genius. Kierkegaard draws his concept of genius from Hoffmann and Hegel. Hoffmann held that genius overcame alienation through a work essentially cultural, although Hoffmann's notion of transcendental art appears to embrace all human experience. Kierkegaard, too, thinks genius pre-eminently a cultural figure who 'humanely educates men in Christianity, transforming the many into the individual'.

Hegel gave genius a cultural and a political character, on the one hand as transcendental epistemologist and, on the other, as world-historical individual: who, however, since he must know what is 'in the age', is something of an epistemologist himself. Hence Kierkegaard's genius, though in a sense an 'educator', is engaged in a world-historical struggle against political liberalism.

Kierkegaard's genius also resembles the world-historical individual in his relationship to the ethical. Just as the world-historical individual stands outside the unequivocal ethical sphere of the existent, while the rest of mankind belongs solely to that sphere, Kierkegaard's extraordinary or special individual belongs to an ethically ambiguous religious sphere, while normal individuals remain in the ethical sphere. Hence Kierkegaard's use of 'religion' to signify the true, the higher demonism of his own system, which is founded upon 'The edification which rests in the thought that as against God we are always wrong.'

Hence too Kierkegaard's assertion that 'in a certain sense there resides infinitely more good in the demonic than in the trivial man'; and hence his efforts, especially in *Fear and Trembling* to identify within the religious 'a teleological suspension of the ethical'. For in *Fear and Trembling* Kierkegaard insists that, whether Abraham is a man of God or merely a madman, he remains a man who intends murder—and that this point is annulled by religion.

In *Repetition* Kierkegaard calls his concept of demonic genius 'the legitimate exception'. The exception's relationship to the universal is the paradox developed by Hegel. The genius is against the universal because he destroys the present moment or existent of the universal; but he is also for it because he establishes a new and higher phase of the universal. The demonic God who either is, or manifests himself through, the universal strives with the genius as legitimate exception to the universal.

The legitimate exception is like one lost and found, who causes the angels more rejoicing than do all the ninety-and-nine of bourgeois normality: he is the sinner who is higher than the just. Yet he must also bend under the menacing greatness of his world historical task, he must suffer precisely because he is who he is. In *Repetition* Kierkegaard sees demonic genius as a wrestling Jacob who must contend with a demonic God and prevail. 'The whole is a wrestling match', declares Kierkegaard, 'in which the universal breaks with the exception, breaks with it in conflict, and strengthens it through this contest.'

But Kierkegaard's existential genius, like Hoffmann's genius, must strive not only with the higher, transcendental demonism but also with the lower demonism of the present alienated order. He is like the driver of a wagon to which are harnessed two ill-matched horses, one the winged Pegasus of infinity, the other the worn-out hack of the temporal. Until his work is done, such genius must suffer exclusion from the universal for, though the *legitimate* exception, he is still the exception, who must stand outside and against the universal until its new, transcendental phase is realised.

And genius cannot be certain who he is. For he

must be especially conscious of the divisions within himself, and must always fear whether the element of the one within him has not been so subordinated to the element of the many that he has become simply the philistine imitation of genius, the 'false extraordinary', the 'illegitimate exception'.

Thus Kierkegaard expected genius to suffer, and did himself suffer. But he did not accept that genius would be a hero, suffering perhaps but suffering merely incidentally to his work. Kierkegaard thought that existential genius must suffer because he must be a martyr. At the age of 22 Kierkegaard hoped to 'find the idea, for which I will live and die'. Eighteen years later, in 1853, he claimed always to have thought 'that men are given whose destiny is to be sacrificed in one way or another, to be sacrificed for others to forward the idea—and that I with my special cross was such a man.'

Kierkegaard held various ideas about the objective character of the martyrdom he thus envisaged for himself. On the one hand, he often interpreted his renunciation of marriage as martyrdom. On the other hand, from 1846 onward he tended either to regard the *Corsair* episode as his martyrdom or to expect a similar event to destroy him at a future date. Finally, after 1848, when Kierkegaard directly opposed the authorities of church and state, he hoped or feared that his final break with them would lead to legal persecution. When he published his first article against Mynster, Kierkegaard wrote, 'Certainly what has occupied me through all the recent period was what God willed that I should do, and the idea that I should stake all on causing a catastrophe, on being arrested, tried, executed if possible.'

These desires for destruction could be attributed to Kierkegaard's character; but a more significant cause is the romantic masochism which encouraged Kierkegaard's character to develop as it did. Martyrdom had been viewed as a way to the transcendental at least since the appearance of *Werther*, forty years before Kierkegaard's birth.

Hegel played a great part in these developments, yet Kierkegaard strove to move beyond what he regarded as Hegel's vulgarly ethical concerns to a truly amoral and demonic concept of religion, and therefore of existence. The world-historical individual's martyrdom restored him to the ethical by punishing his crimes. Kierkegaard emphasised the reward rather than the punishment of genius: thus Abraham the man who intends murder has his son restored to him, Job has his possessions doubled. Admittedly Kierkegaard's notion of the existential subjectivity which is genius's transcendental reward must look much like punishment to most: but that is a necessary element in Kierkegaard's thorough-going demonism.

Martyrdom ultimately arises from the modernist, demonic concept of the trancendental. The one must suffer because only in suffering can he achieve existential subjectivity. The *Concluding Unscientific Postscript* claims that 'the faith of the religious man is precisely that in suffering there is life', for 'to exist essentially'—that is, to be religious, in Kierkegaard's sense—'is intensity and the action of intensity is suffering.'

Martyrdom also arises from Kierkegaard's idea of 'humanely' educating men to be existentially subjective. For Kierkegaard assumes that genius must suffer because only by suffering can he teach others of the 'terrors of existence' concealed by the complacency of philistine spiritlessness. Martyrdom's educational character is seen especially in Kierkegaard's idea of the 'witness to the truth'. The witness not only states but proves the truth, and proves the truth not objectively, by argument or evidence, but subjectively by self-sacrifice. The witness, argued Kierkegaard, would invite men to compel him to deny his doctrine; and when he suffered, and indeed died, the doctrine would triumph. Kierkegaard wished genius to teach with his head in the noose, since only if he was hanged would his lesson subjectively be learned.

## Existentialism and philistinism

Because Kierkegaard used Christianity for his own purpose—even though these were far removed from the Christian tradition—his ideas have been interpreted as though they belonged to conventional modern religion, with its strong liberal and humanitarian elements. This mistake leads some people to attribute to Kierkegaard a 'humanity' foreign to him. It is held, for example, that he addresses his doctrine of existential subjectivity to 'man' without qualification. But Kierkegaard is a profound inegalitarian who

assumes that the many stand farther from the seriousness of the 'tasks of existence' than does the one.
Hence the possibility of existential subjectivity is
revealed to the one precisely because he is less of the
many than are the many; and this possibility is
revealed to the many, if at all, only secondarily and
through the one.

Indeed all that Kierkegaard writes of existential
subjectivity is calculated to repel the great majority
of men. It is a way of life inseparable from suffering, a
confrontation with a demonic God whose presence
may drive men mad. Certainly Kierkegaard does
speak of 'eternal happiness', but he does so rather less
often than either his Christian or his romantic predecessors—and he attributes to happiness what many
would think a singularly curious significance.

Kierkegaard envisages for the many at best a subjectivity that establishes them not in the religious sphere,
the sphere of a direct relationship with the absolute,
but in the ethical sphere, the sphere where men exist
as normal individuals in immediate unity with the
universal. The young Kierkegaard believed that world
history would introduce a new period in which 'the
individual stands for nothing as such, but everything
as a link in the chain.' It is as links in the chain, as
'normal' individuals, who exist only to reproduce the
universal in themselves, that the many enter the higher
realm, if they enter it at all. Genius was to destroy the
many therefore—even if he was to reconstitute the
mass as individuals. 'A single man, good God, what is
a single man against the many', wrote Kierkegaard, 'and

yet a single man, only one single man is used to explode the many, the millions.'

Kierkegaard demanded from men seriousness, passion and faith. Philistine imitation of existential subjectivity and existential genius must discredit and destroy these qualities. But Kierkegaard had to teach his doctrine if men were to know the ideal of existential subjectivity; and the more thoroughly and the more successfully that doctrine was taught, the more easily philistinism could appropriate it.

For, Kierkegaard observed, if a man proclaimed 'with unction and pathos' the doctrine that no one should have disciples, 'he would be understood and soon ten would announce themselves seeking to preach this doctrine, merely for a free shave once a week.' Kierkegaard proposed to escape such humiliation by becoming as 'unrecognisable' as 'a policeman is in plain clothes': in other words, he would teach his doctrine esoterically.

Hamann had brought romantic esotericism to a high level of development and Kierkegaard paid Hamann the tribute of using, as the epigraph to *Fear and Trembling*, Hamann's saying, 'What Tarquinius Superbus said in his garden with the poppies his son understood, but not the messenger.' Tarquinius, by striking off the poppy-heads, told his son—but not the runner who reported this deed—to execute the elders of Gabii. So, too, Kierkegaard hoped to address his transcendental doctrine to the one, but to remain incomprehensible to the philistine many. In short, he proposed to write only for what, in *Repetition*, he called his 'true reader'.

Kierkegaard's books seek to follow Hamann's esoteric example. They are often pseudonymous, they are always ill-written. Structural devices, such as the boxes within boxes of *Either-Or*, or the irksome typological inventories of *The Concept of Dread*, obscure their significance; while an elaborate and difficult terminology enables the most diverse subjects to be treated in a language at once uniform and clandestine.

Esotericism shapes even Kierkegaard's attitude to *genre*. Kierkegaard did not wish to write philosophy, because that was tainted with objectivity. He condemned 'systems' and cast much of his work in semi-fictional form. But because fiction was popular, he presented character, situation and event in the most arid or abstract fashion possible. Kierkegaard's 'pseudonym' Constantine Constantius remarks that he could improve *Repetition*, by adding detail, scenery and personalities. He concludes, 'this history would thus become a novel two feet thick. That I do not care to do. I do indeed eat lettuce but I always eat the heart alone. The leaves, I think, are for the swine.'

Kierkegaard did not stop at literary esotericism, for he believed that life itself was a medium highly suitable to the esoteric. He boasted that he convinced all men, by ostentatious and well-timed appearances in the street and at the theatre, that he was entirely idle during the period in which he wrote *Either-Or*. He broke off his engagement in circumstances of elaborate deception; he acted against the *Corsair* in such a way as to conceal as much as he could of his aims and motives; and he designed his intended martyrdom to be an esoteric sign intelligible only to those who truly sought the existential way.

Christianity and existentialism cannot be separated from esotericism in Kierkegaard's doctrine. There was a system to life, he admitted in the *Postscript*, but it was a system known to God, not to Hegel. Salvation can be apprehended only in terms of its mode of acquisition. That mode is faith, which Kierkegaard understood not as assent to doctrine, or performance of ritual act— either of which interpretations would of course admit the objectivity of the many—but as an inexplicable 'leap' of commitment.

No man can recount another's leap, because that would be to objectify, to alienate faith, which each man must experience for himself, existentially and sub- jectively. God, claims the *Postscript*, is like a man with a treasure who excludes the crowd and admits to see it only each man separately. Hence God denies man the estrangement, yet assumed security, of the objective, and requires him to approach his own existence sub- jectively.

Kierkegaard interprets Christianity thus in order to express his own esoteric existentialist doctrine. Existen- tialism, reasons Kierkegaard, means the search for a transcendental state of existential subjectivity. 'Direct communication', the discourse of the world of objec- tivity—the language of science, philosophy or business, for example—must frustrate that search by reducing subjectivity to the objectively comprehensible, on which philistinism thrives. Existential subjectivity demands 'indirect communication', which does not convert existence into an object, available to the philistine many.

Existential subjectivity can be proclaimed only to the individual who seeks it and, in this sense, Kierkegaard believes, existentialism cannot be a doctrine which anyone could study and understand. '*Objectively* WHAT *is said is emphasised, subjectively* HOW *it is said*', declares the *Postscript*. For existential subjectivity is a process of becoming rather than of being, of appropriation rather than possession and, above all, a process which each man must enter upon for himself.

From this idea Kierkegaard did not waver. Yet the paradox of his last work, the articles and pamphlets against Mynster and his church, is that, despite Kierkegaard's esoteric intent, he achieved through these writings a greater fame, and especially among the many, than he had ever known before. What Kierkegaard designed to be the ultimate polemic against the spiritless philistinism of the present age was presumed by his readers to justify their own vulgar bourgeois irreligion. 'Here in Copenhagen', wrote a pastor of the Danish church to Kierkegaard's brother, 'people drink a glass and say "Damme if Søren Kierkegaard ain't right".' The philistines had triumphed once more.

# 4

## THE MODERNISM OF WYNDHAM LEWIS

### *Philistia*

'THE artist in England has his being upon a precarious beach-head in Philistia', claimed Percy Wyndham Lewis. From this dispiriting domain, he suspected, art was about to be evicted as decisively as the British from Dunkirk. For the century between Kierkegaard's birth in 1813 and the appearance of Lewis's manifesto *Blast* in 1914 had seen the rapid expansion and consolidation of the philistinism that both men feared.

Lewis read Kierkegaard only in 1943 but studied Hoffmann and Dostoevsky before the First World War. Such reading confirmed Lewis's belief that the human community was merely a 'congeries of parasites subsisting upon The Individual', the one in whom all higher values reside. The many, the human parasites, did not thank the one, against whom in fact they waged permanent 'herd-war'.

That war expressed itself throughout society and culture. Hence the analysis applied to *Moby Dick* by Michael Kell-Imrie, hero of Lewis's novel *Snooty Baronet*. Captain Ahab 'stood for Numbers', concluded Kell-Imrie, and the hunted white whale for 'the One over against the Many'. In *Moby Dick* the one wins. But in world history the many triumphed, because social, political and economic change transferred power from the educated, the intelligent and the vital to the mediocre and alienated masses.

*The Art of Being Ruled* (which Lewis planned to call *The Politics of Philistia*) traced this transfer of power to the enlightenment. Before the enlightenment, society retained its organic unity and each man preserved his self, however humble. After the enlightenment every man aspired to be '*l'homme éclairé*', in which abstract ideal he lost both himself and his place in society. And from this abstract ideal came the spurious common culture and the subversive common humanity upon which democracy was built.

Though the romantics challenged the enlightenment, they merely served, Lewis believed, to further what the enlightenment had begun, since, despite esoteric technique, they surrendered their doctrine to the philistines. In this respect Lewis compared the romantics to Nietzsche, 'the archetype of the vulgariser', who addressed himself to 'the Superman', but allowed his message to get 'into the hands of the many'.

In *Murr* Johannes Kreisler had feared that 'the good people who are bad musicians, or rather no musicians at all' would imitate and debase the 'aesthetic love' of the 'real musicians'. The Germans' romantic sentimentality, their suicidal 'welt-schmerzen', predisposed them to realise Kreisler's forebodings, according to Lewis. His first novel, *Tarr*, therefore turns *Murr* on its head. Johannes Kreisler becomes Otto Kreisler, the displeasing Prussian philistine in whose 'fantastic arrogance' the 'Martinet and the Coquette are mingled'. So far from elevating sexuality into transcendental art, Otto Kreisler debases art into a superstitious and concupiscent notion of 'Woman'; he practices world renunciation by marrying his fiancée to his father; and he invokes the forces of genius only to commit ludicrous rape, incompetent murder and despicable suicide.

Murr, on the other hand, is transformed into the real artist Tarr, a 'neo-classicist' to whom even the true romantic, untainted with philistinism, is 'permanently intoxicated' by his transcendental vision of greatness and perfection; while the romantic philistine is merely an estranging and ignoble revolutionary. 'The "classical"', writes Lewis, 'stood for the "old order", tradition and authority, the "romantic" for the new insurgent life of the popular imagination, the self-assertion of the populace.'

Enlightenment and romanticism—or at least philistine romanticism—together produced political democracy. Lewis preferred another political system. 'The fierce opposition of the principles of democracy or liberalism on the one hand, and dictatorship on the other,' he wrote in *The Art of Being Ruled*, 'resolves itself into the secular question of the One and the Many: of a unification of the world or a plurality of control: of the rule of the minority or the majority; rule by show of hands or rule by the most vigorous and intelligent.' In the world to which Lewis addressed himself, 'show of hands' seemed to have won the day.

Lewis used much of his criticism and his fiction to analyse the modern world. He particularly concerned himself with race, the conflict between generations, and, above all, with what Lewis called the 'sex war'. Feminism represented, he believed, an attack by inferiority upon superiority; while homosexuality destroyed male authority and intellect, depersonalised humanity and emasculated man. Lewis linked these phenomena: 'The "Homo" is the child of the "Suffragette"', he argued.

But woman was a greater threat than homosexuality, for it was merely a sham, while she was the hard, alien reality of bourgeois sentimentality, deadening materialism and drive to multiplicity. 'How foul and wrong this haunting of women is!' exclaims Tarr. '— They are everywhere. — Confusing, blurring, libelling, with their half-baked, gushing, tawdry presences! It is like a slop of children and the bawling machinery of the inside of life, always and all over our palaces.'

Like many romantics, Lewis assumed that art could introduce a new and higher order; and hence he particularly feared the philistine campaign against art. When society cannot 'overcome' a 'great creation or invention of art', wrote Lewis in *Time and Western Man*, the work is instead 'accepted. Its canonisation is its martyrdom. It is at all events robbed of its effect by a verbal acquiescence and a little crop of coarse imitations.'

In an earlier, more human world, Lewis believed, art acted directly upon all men; but the modern, alienated world confined knowledge of art to a few self-appointed experts, who used it as material for their pseudo-art of criticism. Meanwhile the vulgar many, without actually painting or writing anything, took 'studios', cultivated art gossip and pretended to be artists.

Philistines degraded romanticism into 'bohemianism'. *Tarr* mocks Fräulein Liepmann and her 'bourgeois bohemian' circle, the chief member of which is Tarr's fiancée Bertha Lunken, whose false artiness ranges from her vile ideas of décor to the cheap romanticism that leads to her rape by Kreisler. Bohemia and allied regions of Philistia ultimately produced what Lewis's novel *The Apes of God* terms 'The Ape of God proper', the affluent philistine 'amateur of some or of all arts'. The ape of God mocked the divine gift of genius, made a monkey of the deity, and tried to substitute for the transcendental aspirations of the one the estranging worldliness of the many.

Lewis emphasised the extremism of these 'new Philistines'. The old philistine copied romantic painting with essentially timid, and manifestly bourgeois, representations of purple heather, shaggy cows or rollicking monks; and imitated great literature with homely, sentimental or comic novels and pallid or whimsical poetry. The new philistines abandoned such caution for a 'revolutionary' attempt to be more advanced than the most daring genius. Lewis accused Pound, Joyce and Eliot of appealing to this 'revolutionary' movement; and above all he charged the magazine *transition* with a 'feverish "diabolism"' which attempted to revive the '*romantic* point of view' in the form of 'a New Philistinism (smeared over with a debased intellectualist varnish)'.

Though Lewis's own work shows a definite surrealist

influence, he grouped surrealism with the new philistinism. He condemned surrealism as 'a sort of revenge
of the second-rate' which, by exploiting the ludi-
crously horrific, and the horrifically ludicrous, discred-
ited all but the least ambitious art. 'The unorthodox
became associated fatally in the public mind with
the clownish', claimed Lewis—who sold few of his
own pictures to a British public that, so far from adopt-
ing the 'revolutionary' tastes of Bohemia, thought him
far too difficult.

Twenty-five years later, however, British artists had
largely caught up with Lewis who proceeded to expose
the philistine 'extremism' of a new generation. 'Extremism . . .' wrote Lewis in *The Demon of Progress in
the Arts*, 'is a pathological straining after something
which boasts of a spectacular *aheadofness*—looking upon
the art in question as a *race*.' Thus, he concluded,
Philistia 'hurries an artist to zero and to the death of
talent.'

### *Split self and puppet man*

Lewis regards the self as a 'subtle and multitudinous'
organism, ideally able, however, to contain its own
multiplicity within a unity. But the ordinary human
self is in fact a conflict of 'contradictory things', 'a
meaningless battle of parts', from which unity is absent.
Man seems to find an 'essential ME', amid the oppos-
ing psychological drives of his personality; yet even

this apparent identity is no more than 'the group' of drives 'that has proved the most powerful' in the internal war of being.

In any event, a personal self must exist in, and take to itself, the exterior and of course alien world. 'There is no *you*', writes Lewis, 'apart from what you perceive'. The need to perceive forces upon the self the 'animal duality' of human nature. For without 'the Wild Body and the Primitive Brain', the disembodied self must cease to be: even though these inescapable but unruly companions continually threaten the self's existence.

The social world offers the self other, and perhaps greater, dangers, as Lewis attempted to show in his semi-drama *The Enemy of the Stars*. Arghol, the work's chief character, condemns the social persona, the self existing in the realm of men, as a 'loathsome deformity' got by rubbing against others. '*Anything but yourself is dirt*', claims Arghol. 'Anybody, that is. All people, in their outer contacts, are unclean.'

Humanity seems thus to exist in a more or less permanent estrangement from itself and from the world, quite anterior to those political or cultural developments to which Lewis's predecessors tend to attribute the phenomenon of alienation. Yet the notion of *permanent* estrangement is simply the measure of Lewis's modernist pessimism. For he too finds aliena-tion intensified in modern times, when, for example, the very size of the state makes man a mere particle of a vast crowd, wasted—as the First World War showed —on trivial or futile ends.

Individuals so reduced to the mass acquire a social

and even personal interdependence, foreign to that unalienated realm where men are fully themselves, distinct yet united. This interdependence blurs all personality in an inhuman confusion. 'We all today (possibly with a coldness reminiscent of the insect world) are in each other's vitals—overlap, intersect, and are Siamese to any extent', Lewis claimed.

This inhuman confusion was governed by the manipulations ingenuously described as democracy, the 'Bankers' Olympus' where both bourgeois parliamentarians and left wing agitators were tools of big business. 'The human being was no longer the unit', Lewis warned. The 'mesmeric methods of Advertisement', political as well as economic, had divided man into a 'sequence of ephemeroids', which were then reorganised into 'group rhythms' of collective thought and action. The 'so-called democratic masses' might think themselves sovereign and free, but they were no freer than a donkey in a water wheel.

Modern intellectual developments afforded Lewis other illustrations of estranged reality. Although his own view of the self owed much to modern science, Lewis opposed contemporary biological and psychological theory because it merely sought to prove or even to justify the division of man. 'Inside us also', he wrote, 'the crowds were pitted against the Individual, the Unconscious against the Conscious, the "emotional" against the "intellectual", the Many against the One.' 'Every organism or *Unity* whatever, political social or psychological, has fallen apart in hostile conflict', Lewis concluded.

Much of Lewis's thinking about alienation was shaped by the work of Henri Bergson. Lewis, like Proust or Beckett, admired Bergsonian theory. But Lewis opposed what he admired, to a degree perhaps unparalleled among Bergson's disciples.

Bergson tried to divide the inanimate from the animate by locating these two categories in different temporal worlds. The inanimate existed, according to Bergson, in mere reversible, valueless time, the kind of time in which, for example, chemical elements could first be synthesised into compounds, and then re-separated into their original entities. The animate existed in irreversible duration, which *changed* and indeed evolved what it contained, and to which therefore some life value could be attached. Thus, for instance, man matured as a person, and developed historically, in duration; and each of his successive selves, personal or historical, was produced by duration.

Bergson hoped thus to vindicate man's position in a scientific world. Lewis believed Bergson had *degraded* man however. By dividing subject and object into time-slices, Lewis argued, duration estranged self both from self and from the world. According to such a theory, Lewis warned his readers, '"You" become the series of your temporal repetitions; you are no longer a centralised self, but a spun-out, strung-along series, a pattern-of-a-self, depending like a musical composition on time.'

What duration did to the *subject* it must also do to any *object* that was to be found in duration. Bergson, claimed Lewis, substituted for objects 'a cluster of "events" or of perspectives which shade off into each other.' Bergson deprived the self of the exterior world necessary to its existence as a self, and left only abstract 'scenes' which 'flourish phantasmally' before the estranged and incomprehending subject. In duration, all becomes 'flux', a stream of undifferentiated 'life' that submerges personality and swamps cognition.

Bergson also offended Lewis by dividing phenomena, including man, into two elements, deadening matter and creative *élan vital*. Phenomena, thus considered, are mixtures of these two elements, ranging from man, in his relative abundance of *élan vital*, at one extreme, to inanimate objects, virtually lacking *élan vital*, at the other. Lewis interpreted the notion of *élan vital* as a form of romantic nature worship, vitalising the natural order, while denying man all distinction from the inanimate.

In *Time and Western Man* Lewis uses the term 'time philosophy' to treat Bergson's different though related ideas about time and *élan vital* as one unified system. This usage allows Lewis the paradox of arguing that time philosophy reduces man both to a fluid series of time-slices moving in the temporal flux, and, simultaneously, to a rigid dead mechanism. According to Lewis, time philosophy infallibly tends 'to transform the living into a machine', because Bergsonian vitalism assumes a continuum between man and machine, animate and inanimate, living and dead.

For while a machine is a piece of vitalist life, aroused from its apparent lifelessness by the presence of however small a quantity of *élan vital*, vitalist life, suffused by matter, is as dead as a machine. Lewis's essay 'Super-nature versus the Super-real' observes that 'A machine in violent motion ceases to look like a machine. It looks, perhaps, like a rose, or like a sponge.' Conversely, of course, in Bergsonian theory, a rose or a sponge looks like a machine. And if this is so, then man too, is a lifeless mechanism which the time philosophy despises. 'I like to see a few corpses about,' Lewis makes the time philosopher Bailiff say in *The Childermass*, 'it makes the others seem almost alive.'

Lewis represents lifeless humanity as 'split selves' or 'split-men'. His paintings, drawings and book designs contain a series of such split selves, perhaps best represented by the ingenious emblem on the cover of his essay *Count your Dead—They are Alive!* where appears one warlike figure (seemingly brandishing a weapon in each hand), in fact composed of two men (labelled with the hammer-and-sickle and the swastika) fighting each other. Arghol, said to be named autobiographically after the double star Algol or *Alpha persei*, is one of Lewis's earliest literary split-men; and Jamesjulius Ratner of *The Apes of God* is another split-man whom Lewis portrays as a character divided, like Arghol, within himself.

Influenced by Hoffmann, however, Lewis more commonly represents the split self as doubles, always *à deux*, yet always in conflict. Tarr and Kreisler, Arghol and Hanp, Kell-Imrie and Humph, are doubles, set by Lewis in an ambiguous, everchanging relationship.

Just as Hoffmann's novel could be called *Kreisler*, rather than *Murr*, Lewis liked to suggest that *Tarr* should have been called *Otto Kreisler*. Even though 'to all appearance eliminated' from the novel, Tarr, the narrator of *Tarr* assures us, was 'the real central and absorbing figure all along', and Kreisler, 'though propped up in the foreground', was 'of no importance'. So too Kell-Imrie, the snooty baronet, declares of his literary agent Humphrey Cooper Carter, 'Humph is the hero of this story, not me at all.'

These doubles are, in any event, usually indistinguishable. Thus, Tarr—who resembles Kreisler—becomes the father of the dead Kreisler's child; and Kell-Imrie reports of Humph that he so disagreed with the baronet's plans that he 'really became *Snooty* ... I said to him, to all intents and purposes, "Listen! It is *I* who am Snooty, not you! You keep to your role, and leave *mine* to *me*!"

Hoffmann and other romantics characterised alienated men as puppets as well as doubles. Goethe, observed Lewis, 'divided people into *Puppets* and *Natures*. He said the majority of people were machines, playing a part.' But Lewisian puppet men are derived from the romantic tradition via Bergson's theory of comedy. Bergson argued that laughter preserved men from the rigidity with which matter always threatened them. Whenever men ceased to develop the flexibility and evolutionary adaptability of their *élan vital*, whenever they became stiff and mechanical in thought, word or deed, the comic intervened to warn them of their fate.

Lewis's puppet men manifest a Bergsonian rigidity often symbolised by lameness. Kell-Imrie, and Percy Hardcaster in *The Revenge for Love*, both lose a leg in war; second-lieutenant Thomas Blenner of 'The Crowdmaster' breaks his leg in a fall; and Hyperides, the Bailiff's opponent in *The Childermass* and *The Human Age*, limps. All these figures are sinking rapidly into the foreign and rigid world of earth, from whose estranging deathliness only a mocking laughter calls them back.

## *Inimical genius*

Though romantic transcendentalism originally proposed to raise all men to equal perfection, romantics soon denied that men could become equally perfect, and adopted the doctrine that, just as men are unequal now, they can become perfect only in their inequality. Lewis accepted this doctrine and emphasised the need to control the many, now and in the future; and for this reason preferred continental European totalitarianism to the indiscipline and indirection of the insular democratic tradition. 'I am not a communist; if anything I favour some form of *fascism* rather than communism', he wrote in 1926. 'Nevertheless, when two principles are opposed, and one of these is that of English liberalism, in most cases I should find myself on the other side, I expect.'

Not merely did Lewis wish to see men disciplined,

he also believed that they should be segregated, partly to protect the higher from the lower and partly to fit all men to their proper sphere. Indeed he held that those who desired 'the "lower" or animal life' should be separated from those who chose 'the active, the intelligent life'; that the backward mass should be separated from the educated few; and that women should be separated from men.

Because Lewis required such discipline and segregation in the transcendental as well as the present order, he saw transcendental personality as the enemy of those to be disciplined and segregated: that is, the many. Lewis's early piece, 'The Code of a Herdsman', tells the herdsman genius to protect the 'sacred hill', the 'volcanic heaven', against the philistine herd: '*There are very stringent regulations* about the herd keeping off the sides of the mountain. In fact your chief function is to prevent this happening.'

Tarr believed that 'all effectual men are always the enemies of every time', and his creator tried to find inimical genius both in history and in contemporary Europe. Lewis admired absolutist and medieval monarchy as the tyranny necessary to the discipline and hence the life of the community. 'The feudal european king', wrote Lewis in his book *The Lion and the Fox*, 'was essentially . . . a stranger and an *enemy*'.

The weakness of modern constitutional monarchy, where the king certainly was not such an enemy, and Lewis's aversion to democratic politicians, encouraged him to seek new realisations of genius as enemy. He found what he sought in Hitler, on whom he wrote two books: *Hitler*, which appeared two years before the Nazis gained power, and *The Hitler Cult*, published in 1939.

In the first of these books Lewis argued that Hitler would abolish the social divisions caused and exploited by politicians and big business. In the racially purified state, the 'Class-person', 'a featureless infantile Robot', formed by these divisions, would find himself and his place (whether high or low) through the harmony of Aryan unity. Meanwhile, Hitler, an 'ascetic of Politics' whose austerity was 'not without its nobility', would destroy the corrupt and alien Bohemia of Berlin, with its homosexuality, its Jewish underworld, and its nigger dances; and he would introduce a new discipline heralded in the 'personal neatness' and 'clear blue eyes' of the young Nazis.

Lewis later claimed that he had misunderstood Nazism. 'The "heads will roll" phrase is typical', he admitted in *The Hitler Cult*. 'I did not take it seriously when first I heard it: I supposed it to be a picturesque schoolboy jargon.' But although there was much that seems ill-considered and naïve in what Lewis wrote in 1931, Hitler's substantive relevance to Lewis's ideas does not rest upon misconception. Lewis sought, and found, in Hitler an example of the concept of genius, and above all the concept of genius as the enemy of philistinism, of the estranging many.

Genius possessed the highest human qualities, as did Hitler, in however perverted a form. Genius added to his specifically human qualities the power of fate or of destiny. He was indeed, in this sense, a world-historical figure, like Hitler. Above all, genius overcame the human crisis and introduced a transcendental realm; and this programme Hitler offered to fulfil in a European 'new order' centred upon the Germanic 'thousand-year Reich'. That Hitler was, if genius, clearly demonic genius merely brought romantic demonism to a practical conclusion.

In *The Hitler Cult* Lewis argued that 'Winkelmann, Goethe, Hölderlin, Kant or Hegel have no more to do with the entourage of Herr Hitler than they have to do with the Esquimaux of Coronation Gulf.' But these representatives of German and indeed European romanticism had developed the notion of alienation, the ideology of genius, which gave intellectual and emotional shape, if not to the Eskimos, at least to Hitler and his movement.

Yet Hitler was sufficiently plebeian to be no genius at all but merely a skilful philistine imitation. *The Hitler Cult* seemed to conclude that Hitler was a philistine. 'Hitler is an incorrigible German romantic', wrote Lewis. 'But it is important to emphasise that he is a romantic of a vulgar order. He is not a *great* romantic—he is not a Schiller. He is more like a dreamy-eyed hairdresser, who reads Schiller, without understanding him, in between haircuts.'

Lewis's earlier defence of Hitler as inimical genius nevertheless cost him what amounted to ostracism in England, and may have been a major factor in his virtual exile in north America during the Second World War.

If so the man you are that lets the cat
Out of the bag, you're a marked fellow and that's
   flat

Lewis wrote in 1933.

Lewis took his own advice in other works, where he confined himself to theoretical and literary presentation of transcendental personality. Lewis's imaginative portrait of inimical genius shows him to be as neat as a young Nazi: 'Tarr's white collar', for example, 'shone dazzlingly in the sun. His bowler hat bobbed and cut clean lines as he spoke.'

Inimical genius may be a martial fascist, like Hyperides in *The Childermass* and Starr-Smith in *The Apes of God*; but more often he is simply a soldier like Kell-Imrie, the veteran who studies 'the psychology of the Samurai caste', and Ker-Orr the 'soldier of humour' of *The Wild Body*. Inimical genius may also be a policeman. Thus Kell-Imrie says of his human typology, 'my portraits do partake of the criminal dossier. I *am* forced to do a good deal of detective work ... I *am* slightly policemanesque!'

Both *Snooty Baronet* and *Tarr* describe calamities provoked by the almost unconscious but fatal power of the one. Kell-Imrie's thoughtless, but effective, 'big pointed yawns' drive the low-grade fashionable poet and self-taught matador Ron McPhail to prove his manhood by fighting the bull which kills him. When Tarr talks about Anastasya Vasek, he drives Otto Kreisler—who is, unknown to Tarr, her admirer—to the frenzy in which he murders his rival Soltyk and then hangs himself. 'There is a point in life', observes the narrator, 'beyond which we must hold people responsible for accidents and their unconsciousness. Innocence then loses its meaning. Beyond this point Tarr had transgressed.'

Innocence soon passes over into conspiracy. 'What I suppose I was doing', Kell-Imrie remarks, 'was to hatch a plot against Mankind.' This plot characteristically takes a violent form. Kell-Imrie finally shoots Humph twice in the back. 'Of all the shots I have ever fired, at all the game I have ever hunted (and this includes the hippo)', declares the baronet, 'I don't believe that any shot ever gave me so much pleasure as that second one. ... Indeed it is fair to say I think that I shall never lose that pleasant feeling of immediate satisfaction. ... A thing of beauty is a joy for ever! That second one was a beauty!'

Kell-Imrie's ecstasy does not exhaust what Lewis has to say about inimical genius. Indeed triumph is much less important than suffering to Lewis's modernist picture of genius. 'Was Napoleon successful in his life, or did he ruin himself and end his days in miserable captivity?' asks Tarr in Hegelian mood. '— *Passion* precludes the idea of success. Worldly failure is its condition.'

Lewis expected the vengeful many to frustrate whoever attempted to disturb their deathly philistine calm. Tyrants of normality reappear throughout Lewis's life: Roger Fry, the arbiter of art fashion, with whom Lewis quarrelled as early as 1913; Arnold Bennett, arch-reviewer of the inter-war years, who kept Lewis 'in a spiritual concentration camp—of barbed silence'; and above all the Royal Academy, 'that crushing and discouraging symbol of malignant and arrogant mediocrity', whose hostility towards Lewis culminated in rejection of his portrait of T. S. Eliot in 1938.

If the many persecuted genius, who alone could overcome their alienation, his task itself demanded that the transcendental personality must suffer. 'To produce is the sacrifice of genius', Tarr declares of the artist. And genius fares no better than ruler. 'The life of the ruler . . .', Lewis wrote, 'will be severe. . . . To be a true ruler', Lewis concludes, 'he will have paid every penalty of man's aspiring lot, a pact with the Devil included.'

Lewis expressed the demonism of suffering inimical genius in a series of drawings of the uncanny—from 'Witch on Cowback' to 'Walpurgisnacht'—which he produced in north America during the nineteen-forties. These studies, and the contemporaneous, visually related 'Lion' drawings, provide the symbolism of a transcendental personality that scourges alienating normality, but thus suffers, and becomes demonic.

Suffering demonic genius is not necessarily a martyr however. Lewis's portrait of Naomi Mitchison, finished in 1939, includes a sketch of the crucifixion behind the sitter's right arm. This motif persists at least until the 'Small Crucifixion Series' of 1941, that is, through Lewis's last months in pre-war England and his first years in exile. But if Lewis used the crucifixion to represent genius' martyrdom, his modernist pessimism set limits to such romantic ideas.

A sketch of the nineteen-forties juxtaposes the cruci-
fied martyr-saviour, and Don Quixote, the futile
victim; while a companion sketch shows Quixote and
an open book listing the titles of Lewis's chief works.
Since these Quixotes use motifs from the drawings of
witches, Lewis seems to unite the romantic concept of
the martyr, and the modernist concept of the victim,
with their common factor of demonism.


## Visions of death and hell

Lewis's modernist concept of genius as victim cannot
be separated from his idea of the transcendental.
Romantics contrasted the darkness of this alienated
world with the glorious light of another dispensation.
Man might find himself in hell, but he could still fly
to heaven. The practical and intellectual difficulties of
this doctrine changed romanticism into modernism,
which afforded no prospect of paradise, which doubted
the possibility of the transcendental and which reinterpreted the transcendental as suffering.

Transcendentalism becomes 'descendentalism', so to
speak: a system in which alienation is resolved, if at all,
into a condition so sombre and forbidding that only the
very greatest can endure it. The nineteenth century
produced many such descendental systems. From these
systems has developed the modernist consciousness
which, while recognising to the full the alienation of
the world, utterly doubts the possibility of escaping

from alienation and assumes that most will prefer the prison of alienation to the hypothetical escape therefrom. And ultimately modernism contrasts the alienated and the transcendental (or descendental) conditions simply as realms of life and of significance, in the former of which men merely live their estranged lives, and in the latter of which they know the significance of their alienation.

The transition from romanticism to modernism raises what Lewis calls a 'very fundamental question'. In *Time and Western Man* he expresses this question as the alternatives 'whether we should set out to transcend our human condition . . . or whether we should translate into human terms the whole of our datum.'

The 'whole of our datum' indicates that life is death: and death is life. That alienated life ever tends to death is an axiom of Lewis's critique. Hence philistine extremism brings the 'death of talent'; estranged man is a puppet who displays the mechanical rigidity of death; and even genius appears as a deathly victim. But paradoxically death also represents the state beyond alienation towards which Lewis looks.

This paradox partly arises from ideas particularly associated in Britain with Pater and aestheticism. Pater regarded men, in the state of restless 'physical life', as a mere 'combination of natural elements', or, anticipating Bergson, as a flux 'infinitely divisible in time'. Pater trusted that this fragmentation would be transcended in death: in the 'venerable beauty' seen in the sepulchre in Cecilia's house in *Marius*, for example, or in the 'extreme purity of the outlines' of Emerald Uthwart's corpse. But the corpse is nevertheless a dynamic system in which restless life, of a lower order, continues to manifest itself through the phenomena of decomposition. Pater's disciples therefore sought another symbol of their transcendental ideal; and they found this in the deathly unity of the mask or the statue.

With these ideas Lewis was entirely familiar. Hence the analysis of the relationship between art and death in his 'Essay on the Objective of Art in our Time'. Firstly, argues Lewis, art reckons with, or renders into significance, the deadening and estranging materiality of a Bergsonian world. 'In our bodies we have got already so close to extinction' that art's chief task is to express this extinction. In art, Lewis suggests, 'The game consists in *seeing how near you can get*, without the sudden extinction and neutralisation that awaits you as matter, or as the machine'.

Secondly, art works upon the world of death by raising that world to a higher, an aesthetic death. Lewis appeals to Schopenhauer's 'eloquent and resounding' claim that art 'pauses at this particular thing: the course of time stops: the relations' of life 'vanish from it: only the essential, the idea, is its object'.

Lewis believes that 'the great work of plastic or pictorial art' does precisely this. 'It "pauses at this particular thing"' in the flux of deathly life, and confers upon it 'a sort of immortality'. 'It is an immortality', Lewis concludes, for which the thing immortalised must pay 'with death, or at least with its coldness and immobility.'

Lewis first made his reputation as a painter not by immortalising the physical but by creating what purported to be an altogether unrepresentational world of geometrical abstraction. But he complemented, and then replaced, strict geometrical abstractionism with a more concrete abstractionism inspired by the masks and statues which delighted the cubists. Lewis probably came to these masks and statues very much as a painter but he worked up his painterly enthusiasm into a theory which he derived from the work of Wilhelm Worringer.

Worringer contributed, to Lewis's response both to cubism and aestheticism, the doctrine of *Starrheit*, that is, of an aesthetic rigidity, that parallels the rigidity of material life just as aesthetic deadness parallels the deathliness of material life. Lewis acknowledged his debt to Worringer in the name of his character Starr-Smith and probably also in his conversion of Murr into Tarr.

In any event Tarr propounds the doctrine of transcendental *Starrheit*. 'Anything living, quick and changing, is bad art, always . . .' claims Tarr. 'The shell of the tortoise, the plumage of a bird, makes these animals approach nearer to art . . . *deadness* is the first condition of art.' The dead line of aesthetic rigidity could be found in the cubists' primitive mask forms which Lewis himself used in several of his pictures of the early nineteen-tens. Because the statue is even more rigid than the mask, he also attempted to represent the three-dimensional concept of sculpture in the two dimensions of a picture. The statue, as Tarr put it, has no 'little egoistic fire' of life inside, but 'lives soul-lessly and deadly by its frontal lines and masses'. Lewis pursued a sculptural ideal in the giant torsos of his work before 1914, in his war paintings, and also in later studies of men in armour such as 'The surrender of Barcelona' of 1936.

But Lewis most successfully applied Worringer's doctrine of rigidity in the drawing of 1911 entitled 'Smiling woman ascending a stair'. This work adds to a structure largely reliant upon Picasso the character-istic Lewisian grin, whose display of teeth reveals the deadest and most mask-like element of the natural face. Although Lewis virtually abandoned this motif during the First World War, he returned to it in 1920–1921 when he produced his series of grinning 'tyros'; and from these he developed the totem or mummy-like column figures, which begin with works such as 'Tyro Madonna' of 1921, and continue to Lewis's very last drawings, such as 'Red Figures Carrying Babies and Visiting Graves', finished in 1951.

Lewis used these visions of death to express the elaborate modernist paradox, in which transcendental (or descendental) art separates itself from alienated life; yet in which that art serves to explicate—and therefore to reproduce—alienated life. And that life is now presented as a realm of significance where men's one disastrous victory, if even that can be achieved, is to know themselves for what they are.

But Lewis also sought to represent the descendental

in the notions of hell into which his ideas of death finally merged. One of Lewis's most important paintings now hangs in the National Gallery of Victoria, Melbourne. This picture, probably inspired in part by the Spanish civil war, was first exhibited in 1937 as an example of what Lewis called 'tragic art'. Reddish-brown round-headed figures, fearfully yet inescapably human, appear to tumble in violence out of brilliant red smoke only to fall in agony, madly grinning or merely faceless, into a greyish foreground. The picture bears the title 'Inferno'.

Eyes educated by the abominations of the Second World War may read anachronistic allusions into this scene of hell. Lewis describes the painting as 'a world of shapes locked in eternal conflict . . . superimposed upon a world of shapes, prone in the relaxations of an uneasy sensuality which is also eternal.'

The alternatives which Lewis reads into his visual symbols are aspects of his vision of hell: inimical genius's 'eternal conflict' with the many, to whom it now falls victim, yet against whom it may establish at least a descendental realm of significance; and the eternal 'uneasy sensuality' of acquiescence in the philistine life of the many.

The hell of eternal conflict appears in *The Childermass*, throughout which the Bailiff and his 'contrary pole', Hyperides, 'the oldest opposites in the universe . . . eye each other' across the celestial nightmare which the Bailiff and his masters have constructed out of 'time-stuff'. The Bailiff himself is a Bergsonian object, shifting and fluctuating with time: 'I am

compelled occasionally to modify my appearance',
he explains.

The Bailiff issues passes to the dead men who seek
to cross the river to the allegedly paradisal city which
they can see, but at which it is unlucky even to look.
'You can petition and petition and petition!' the Bailiff
assures the appellants, 'you can do so till you are black
in the face and the worms eat you up. There is practic-
ally no limit to the amount which you can petition.'
Indeed, he admits, 'Many of you have waited months,
some even years, some so long you have ceased to know
since when and have lost count, for your turn to come.'

The paintings of the nineteen-thirties, in which the
round-headed figures of 'Inferno' reappear, develop
the Bergsonian hell of *The Childermass* in different
directions. Pictures such as 'Group of Supplicants',
and 'One of the Stations of the Dead', enclose the
world of *The Childermass* in a fearful darkness of black
and brown, whose momentary reds and blues merely
deepen the terror into which Lewis's round-headed
men—if men they still be—have been plunged. 'The
Mud Clinic', and 'The Tank in the Clinic', on the
other hand, seem to draw upon Lewis's own experience
of illness during the thirties. Round-headed figures
also inhabit the diseased hell of these pictures: they
are stacked away in cupboards by attendants; they
drift like dead men in the sinister clinical tank;
they converse with the skeletons of the dead world
of estranged humanity.

Lewis depicted the eternity of 'uneasy sensuality', a
purely philistine hell, in a great number of drawings

of pseudo-paradises of the many; and these, such as 'Marine Fiesta' of 1942 and 'Negro Heaven' of 1946, are often erotic in character. The hell of philistine sensuality found its literary expression in *Monstre Gai* and *Malign Fiesta*, the two volumes of Lewis's infernal epic, which he published together under the title *The Human Age* shortly before his death. *The Childermass* emphasises the role of Hyperides but *The Human Age* pays renewed attention to James Pullman, who appears in the earlier work, and who is now claimed to be 'the "lone wolf" man, of the fierce modern genius type'.

Pullman, who lives in *le dernier luxe* even in hell, is much more of a philistine than a genius. 'The *Good* and the *Bad* are blurred' in his underworld where God is 'entirely stupid' and Satan predominates. Pullman becomes Satan's chief minister—in which post his sensuality is tempered only by terror—and he advises Satan to annihilate the divine by breeding angels down into men, so that 'There would be everywhere a swarming of ephemeral units in place of a world of larger and more stable things'. Through this diabolical plan, culminating in a fiesta of copulation, hell achieves the age-old philistine goal of making men into spurious gods. Such, Lewis indicates, is the descendental significance of our alienated world.

# 5

## KAFKA AND THE DEFEAT OF GENIUS

### *The urban world*

WHEN Kafka recounted the influences of which he had been conscious while writing the short story 'The Judgement', he mentioned only one of his own earlier writings, the brief piece which appears in his diaries under the title 'The Urban World', a title which identifies the setting of almost all of Kafka's work right up to his death.

For Kafka is, above all, the critic of the urban world. His father was a country Jew, who had migrated to Prague, but whose livelihood, the sale of haberdashery to the villages around the city, kept him and his family on the edge of urban life. Kafka was, therefore, a newcomer to the urban world who relived the revulsion from the city experienced by European intellectuals over and over again since the days of the early romantics, whose works (and especially those of Goethe) Kafka read from his teutophile student days onwards.

The family business, that precarious foothold in the urban world, disgusted Kafka, partly because it was his father's, and partly because it represented the commercial and industrial disorder of the city. But he chose to devote himself to this disorder by taking a job in the Prague Industrial Accident Insurance Institute, where he could study the evils of factory production, and where he could suffer what he felt to be the unhealthy constraints and artificialities of office work.

Kafka deplored intellectual labour as a way of life that separated men from men, and he praised the power of craftsmanship to bring men together. He took lessons in carpentry and, from time to time, practised gardening and farming. Enthusiasm for the concept of an unspoiled and unrestraining natural order over against the regime of the city led him to vegetarianism, nudism and Zionism. But none of these pursuits claimed him completely, because Kafka preferred, for much the greater part of his life, to endure the torments of the urban world.

Despite visits to various European countries, and wide reading in European literature, Kafka retained the outlook not merely of a city dweller but of an Austro-Hungarian, for whom the urban world meant a politically backward and bureaucratic society where the legal-administrative bourgeoisie, created by absolute monarchy, remained pre-eminent. Indeed, as an official of the semi-governmental Industrial Accident Insurance Institute, Kafka belonged to this bourgeoisie.

Hence, though he used bureaucracy and the bureaucratic class to symbolise the order he opposed, Kafka was enough of a bureaucrat to derive considerable pleasure from this symbolic material. He relished the details of desks and telephones; he savoured the style of official communications; and he delighted to portray great bureaucratic institutions such as banks, courts and government departments. The atmosphere of almost all his work suggests the leisurely construction and exegesis of bureaucratic decisions: matters of life and death, no doubt, for those whom they concern, but also the engrossing and recondite vocation of those who prepare them.

Kafka's enjoyment of bureaucratic matters must modify their significance for his critique of the urban world. Furthermore, despite his allegedly left wing youth, Kafka remained loyal to Austria–Hungary, and was dismayed by the Austrian defeats of 1914. Kafka never wrote the overt political satire for which his Czech contemporary Jaroslav Hašek became famous— on the contrary he took pains to avoid it. Thus when Josef K is arrested in what is evidently Habsburg Prague, the narration sharply separates his persecutors from the regime by enquiring, 'who ventured to arrest him at his residence', in 'a constitutional state' where 'peace reigned universal', and 'all the laws stood firm.'

Kafka is said to have thought mankind to be bound in red tape; but his great studies of red tape shun explicit condemnation of the Austro-Hungarian monarchy. For Kafka opposed not the principle of authority embodied in that monarchy, which alone offered central Europe any semblance of historical unity, but rather those more general tendencies of fragmentation, objectification and alienation, from which the system of Habsburg government unfortunately could not be detached.

*The Trial* and *The Castle* attack twentieth-century bureaucracy just as the romantics had attacked the bureaucracies of the eighteenth century, and for approximately the same reasons. But by the twentieth century, central European bureaucracy was no longer a vital force. In some respects it was decayed and corrupt; and the political purposes which it served were—especially in the eyes of the national minorities of Austria–Hungary—oppressive. The alternatives open to the system's critics were revolution, for which Kafka showed little sympathy, or capitalist democracy, with which Kafka acquainted himself quite closely, only to judge it rather more severely than he judged bureaucracy.

America was the great home of capitalist democracy, whither many of Kafka's compatriots emigrated, particularly between 1900 and 1914. 'The Stoker', which Kafka published in 1913, begins with the enforced emigrant Karl Rossmann gazing upon the statue of Liberty in New York harbour. Kafka called the novel of which this piece forms the first chapter *Der Verschollene*, or *Missing Person*. But the later chapters' emphasis so thoroughly shifted from Karl Rossmann's departure from Prague to his experiences in the United States that Kafka's friend, Max Brod, published the book as *America*. Kafka did not re-use his first novel's American setting. But he continued to give notice—for example, in the transatlantic nomenclature of Count *Westwest*, the unseen nobleman in whose domain occurs the action of *The Castle*—that America, symbol of the capitalist urban world, remained his concern.

Kafka interpreted bureaucratic method as a system of enslavement, and such too, he indicated, was the character of capitalism. *America* reveals this enslavement at work in senator Jacob's business where, with 'inhumanly fast and regular' movements, clerks, their heads 'clamped in a band of steel', take down messages amid 'bewildering' noise and 'blazing electric light'.

These robots are entirely alienated from their humanity: just as Kafka was, he claimed, a being destroyed by his work, a man incapable of the unified overview of the world that belongs to complete human personality. 'K had never seen work and life so interwoven as they were here,' reports *The Castle* of K's sojourn in the realm of Count Westwest, 'so interwoven that sometimes it could seem that work and life had changed places'—to the detriment of the human life alienated into an employee pure and simple, reduced to a mere 'hand'.

Alienation of self as employee is a basic theme of 'The Metamorphosis', the story of Gregor Samsa, commercial traveller to a firm organised upon the principle that 'a season for doing no business does not exist at all . . . must not exist.' Gregor accepts this principle; devotes remarkable ardour to his 'exhausting job'; thinks of nothing but his work; never goes out; and briefly entertains himself with the newspapers and a little fretwork. In short, while business flourishes, its slave has ceased to exist—and finally turns into an insect.

The story only hints that the same bizarre mutation awaits all the denizens of the urban world. But 'The Metamorphosis' leaves no doubt that employment dehumanises the employee. When Gregor's father becomes a bank messenger, for example, he receives a livery which he wears even when he sleeps. The man has become a uniform, and his home has been absorbed into his job, just as, in *The Trial*, the court usher resides in the antechamber to the court and, in *The Castle*, the school caretaker must live in the classroom.

Thus far Kafka argues that employment alienates man from himself, by causing him to exist only as employee; and that man is alienated also from the world, towards which he stands, not in a fully human relationship, but in the relationship of a mere passive instrumentality. But no concept of alienation can ignore the problem that, if the many are alienated from themselves and from the world, they usually prefer that alienated condition to the transcendental prospects disclosed by the one. Man's commitment to his own alienation must be explained: and this Kafka does by pointing to the empirical data of the urban world.

The cases of Gregor Samsa and his father show man metamorphosed into subhumanity by capitalist employment. But Kafka knew that, if capitalism tended to treat man only as a unit of labour, it tended to treat him as no more—and therefore emancipated him from the restrictions imposed by earlier social and economic systems, which did have a larger view of man, but which, because of this larger view, imposed upon him many requirements from which capitalist man was free.

Kafka reported that the Czech American 'E.K.', with whom he had a long conversation in December 1914, illustrated this freedom by citing his employers' attitude to his employment, which he began and ended at will because 'they can always use him, though they can always do without him too'. The permissiveness of these employers—apparently the great midwestern mail-order firm Sears, Roebuck—impressed Kafka enough to find its way into his picture both of court and of castle. 'The court wants nothing from you', the chaplain tells Josef K in *The Trial*. 'It receives you when you come and it dismisses you when you go.' The village superintendent of *The Castle* tells K, 'Nobody forces you to stay, but that's certainly not the sack.'

Perhaps this liberality mystifies only the one, for the many seem both to understand and to exploit capitalism's indifference towards man as individual personality. Kafka was baffled and indeed exasperated by the factory girls who turned themselves into machines at their work, and back into women when they left for home; and his fiction reveals his suspicions of such apparent victims of a system which, however, they accept with an equanimity denied to the one.

'The Metamorphosis' openly admits Kafka's mistrust of the many. After Gregor Samsa's transformation, his family endure all the apparent degradations of employment. Mr Samsa becomes a messenger at the bank; Mrs Samsa makes underwear; and their daughter becomes a shop assistant. So long as they remain under Gregor's horrified eye, the Samsas seem demoralised by these calamities; but as soon as he is dead they take a holiday, discuss their admirable jobs and reflect on their attractive prospects.

The urban masses use the freedom which capitalism allows them—if at the price of alienation—to attack the one. The court that accuses Josef K has its offices in the Juliusstrasse, but this street is peopled by the poor who are the new caesars. Kafka first thought to compare the court with a 'socialist rally'. Later, and more skilfully, he interpreted these champions of the poor as 'a local political meeting', representative of the parliamentary system of partisan politics, left and right, whose alleged differences of creed conceal a uniform loyalty to the mob.

## *The sexual underworld*

While the urban world alienates man but emancipates the many against the one, urban culture vindicates the insubordination of the estranged and estranging masses. Modern psychology is an excellent example of this cultural phenomenon: the assailed self tires, as Lewis puts it, of '"independent" individual life' and 'plunges into the Unconscious, where Dr Freud . . . is waiting for him'.

Freud's association with the many may seem paradoxical. For he looked askance upon the libertarian tendencies developed most characteristically in the democratic materialism of America. He feared and condemned the crowd; he regarded women as inferior beings largely bounded by their biological functions; and, perhaps, because he was a physician, he concerned himself first and foremost with man as patient. Above all he attributed humanity's sickness to conflict between the higher values of a civilisation for which, however, he did not greatly care, and the lower values of the sexual instincts.

Freud held that sexuality dominated human beings and expressed itself in everything that they did. 'There is no group of ideas', he wrote in 1911, 'that is incapable of representing sexual facts and wishes': and he catalogued mental and social phenomena accordingly.

Freud converted these notions into a system of misanthropy. He regarded aggression as a prime factor in human life. He interpreted dislikes as repressed desires, whose true meaning only medical science could reveal to self-estranged personality. He discounted art and literature as an elaborate arrangement of genital symbolism. He reduced eroticism to a sexuality realised positively in coitus (which he described as a sadistic act) or negatively in the neurosis and neurasthenia consequent upon repression. In Freud's view man can be an invalid or an animal but never himself: the most he can do is to know what he is through psychoanalysis.

What Freud says of man must be particularly true of the many who are the least human of men. Yet Freud, as understood by Lewis and Kafka, leads the many against the one. He threatens the imperfect contemporary order with revolutionary forces of unconious desire that continually attack both culture and morality, such as these are in the alienated condition. Despite Freudianism's ascetic tendencies, it authorises the worst aspects of philistinism.

For if sexuality is universal, then copulation and

reproduction assume the cosmic proportions of existential human acts. If man is above all a sexual being who needs sexual freedom, sexual prohibitions and constraints should be modified or abolished. If even children have sexual needs and desires, they should be admitted as the equals of adults, whose chief characteristic is sexuality; and among those adults there can be no distinctions more significant than those arising from sexual activity.

Kafka shared Freud's fears. He wrote of 'coitus as punishment', and spoke of love as violence. His sexual life was deeply disturbed. He pursued what he called 'unclean' affairs, such as that with the barmaid Hansi, the steed, he boasted, of whole regiments of cavalry. He was engaged three times, once to Julie Wohryzek, twice to Felice Bauer; he entered into brief relationships with other women notably Milena Jesenska and Dora Dymant; but he never married.

Something of this comes from Kierkegaard who, wrote Kafka, 'bears me out like a friend'. Yet the lengthy analytical letter which Kafka wrote—but never delivered—to his father; the careful accounts of dreams which fill many pages of Kafka's diaries; his self-identification as a neurasthenic; and his plan to 'cure my neurasthenia through my work', that is, through auto-analytical fiction, indicate Freudian rather than Kierkegaardian influence.

Kafka's apparent use of the 'parable' as a genre has been compared with the parabolic method in Freud's treatment of case histories. But Kafka's Freudian fictions draws not so much on rabbinical or scriptural models as on German romance. Such romance appears, in vernacular form, in the Grimms' collection of folk tales and, in literary form, in the romantic *Märchen* (well exemplified in the works of Hoffmann), whose abstruse detail and wealth of dark allusions invite psycho-analysis of the type offered in Freud's *The Interpretation of Dreams*. In a sense Kafka's writings constitute a series of Freudian *Märchen* drawn from the sexual underworld.

'The Judgement', for example, derives its theme of the conflict of father and son from the Oedipus complex and, according to Kafka, was inspired by 'thoughts of Freud, naturally'. Naturally, too, Kafka psycho-analysed the story, which he described as 'a proper birth bedecked with muck and slime'; and he proudly recorded both his sister's comment that the story seemed to be set in the Kafka house, and his own triumphant reply, 'Well, then, father would have to be living in the lavatory.'

Freudian motifs preponderate in Kafka's writing. Thus when Karl Rossmann leaves the ship, on which he has crossed the Atlantic, at the end of the first chapter of *America*, he does so in the company of his alleged uncle senator Jacob. The disembarkation of the senator and the timid boy is drawn, methodologically, direct from Freud. 'The senator put his right hand under Karl's chin, held him tight, pressed himself against him, and stroked him with his left hand', we read. 'Thus they went slowly down step by step' into the boat, in which they rowed rhythmically away over the waves.

Similar symbols appear in *The Trial*. Josef K sheds his clothes and caresses Titorelli who yields to K's requests as if to 'a law of nature'. 'At once', the passage continues, 'they were in the lawcourts' and, with a 'lovely kind of motion', 'sped over the stairs, not simply upwards, but up and down, without any expenditure of effort, as easily as a light boat in water.'

Just as Joyce complained that no one found *Ulysses* funny, Kafka could object that such passages' comic intention has been ignored amid the veneration aroused by his work and personality. Kafka's immediate circle knew better. 'We . . . laughed quite immoderately', recalled Brod, 'when he first let us hear the opening chapter of *The Trial*. And he himself laughed so much that there were moments when he couldn't read any further.'

Kafka's often comic use of Freudian detail creates a picture of a sexual underworld of rampant libido, an underworld in which alienated Freudian man seems to be finally lost. *America* allows Karl Rossmann to escape from the lascivious servant who seduces him, only to fall into the hands first of the homosexual senator Jacob and then successively into those of the creatures of Mr Pollunder's infamous house; of the Hotel Occidental; and of the apartment of the corpulent and promiscuous singer Brunelda.

Moreover, it is a relationship to a woman which connects the heroes of both *The Trial* and *The Castle* to the mysterious institutions which persecute them. Thus, Josef K is arrested in Fräulein Bürstner's bed-room. He finds that 'Lanz', the exceedingly Freudian name of the soldier who seems to be Fräulein Bürstner's protector, is the password into the court. And he finally recognises 'the futility of his resistance' when he sees Fräulein Bürstner as he is being led away to execution.

The new world, the court and the castle are perceived, both by their manifold inhabitants, and by the solitary victim who is drawn towards them, as zones of a truly Freudian sexuality, understood by the one to be both domineering and insubordinate. Romantic and modernist critics represent such estranging regimes as tyrannies of the normality expressed and exerted through agencies such as absolutism, capitalism, or the mundane round of procreation and housekeeping. Particularly during the years 1912–1919 Kafka, not least under Kierkegaard's influence, discovered the tyranny of normality in his father and his fiancée, who together realised the paradoxical sanctions of the Freudian world: the father forever denying the son a manhood the horror of whose inseparable sexuality was endlessly demonstrated by the fiancée.

The fiancée (and, of course, especially Kafka's first fiancée, Felice Bauer) was commemorated by the character and name of Frieda Brandenfeld in 'The Judgement', Fräulein Bürstner in *The Trial* and Frieda in *The Castle*. But Kafka regarded literature chiefly as a means to refine and articulate 'the conflict between fathers and sons': a theme made quite explicit in 'The Judgement', where old Bendemann refuses his son Georg the life, power and pleasures which, the story hints, he intends to keep for himself. 'My writing', Kafka planned to tell his father, 'was all about you.'

The father's tyranny, the tyranny of familial and sexual life, threatens the higher principle of the one with the lower values of multiple human animality. Freud interpreted the sexual element of this animality as a sphere in which desire and disgust, pleasure and pain were inextricably mixed. Even sexual gratification is a form of suffering because the very source of gratification is also the stimulus to shame and remorse. Hence the paradox that symbols of tyranny such as old Bendemann, or the apparatus of the court, typify forces at once libidinous—since the father is nothing if he is not the copulator—and ascetic—because he also personifies conscience or super ego.

If sexuality brings pleasure indivisible from pain, the pleasure itself is a vileness that alienates personality, as is seen in Kafka's gallery of monster women: Johanna Brummer, whose name means meat fly; the immense and seedy Brunelda; the web-fingered Leni, lover of accused men; and Frieda, the barmaid with a whip. A traumatic self-estrangement necessarily arises from the character of man's sexual nature so revealed.

Kafka often uses doubles to express sexual self-estrangement. In *America* Karl Rossmann, infantile but sexual, has a double, still more infantile and sexual (if also drunken and stupid) in Robinson, who brings with him the violent and lustful Delamarche. *The Trial* also introduces a further pair of doubles in the persons of two childish warders: greedy Willem, who eats the breakfast of those he arrests, and the autobiographically named Franz, whose one distinguishing feature is his false claim to a sweetheart. Willem and Franz try to steal Josef K's clothes; are brought into the bank to frighten and disgust him; and may be the two droll executioners who put him to death like a dog. Willem and Franz hypostasise the lower self as entities which 'arrest' Josef K's higher self, just as Robinson and Delamarche eventually imprison Karl Rossmann.

Many intellectual developments predisposed Kafka's generation to consider personality destroyed into a welter of epistemological confusion in which neither self nor world could be known with certainty. Freud's *The Psycho-pathology of Everyday Life*, which first appeared in 1904, relentlessly attributed the epistemological confusion epitomised by the 'Freudian slip' to suppression of psychical material concerning sex or, what in this system is much the same thing, death.

Kafka interpreted nescience and incertitude in Freudian terms. Thus Josef K believes in the 'great power' of women and attempts to involve in his defence Fräulein Bürstner; the court usher's wife; and lawyer Huld's servant Leni. According to the prison chaplain, this is to seek not 'true help' but an 'alien assistance', in whose realm lies confusion and disorder. 'Do you really not see two steps ahead?' asks the priest —and then confuses matters still further by telling, and purporting to expound, the esoteric 'parable of the law' which, Josef K justly complains, makes falsity a 'world principle'.

That falsity *is* a world principle is reaffirmed by *The Castle*. At the beginning of the book the castle itself vanishes into 'an apparent void' from which, in a sense, it does not reappear. K thinks he telephones the castle, but is later informed that there is no telephone connection to that building; and though he seems to work for the castle official Klamm, he does not actually meet his employer.

If he had met him he would not have recognised him for, as Olga explains, not even the villagers know what Klamm looks like. 'A picture of Klamm—which is certainly correct in outline—has been formed from glimpses, from rumours and from many deceptive impulses also', she agrees. 'But only in outline. In other respects the picture varies, and perhaps not so much as Klamm's real appearance varies.'

Furthermore, while K is thought to be in Klamm's employment, he does not do the land surveying for which he is employed—even though Klamm congratulates K on his progress—and in fact he does no work at all. K's fellow employee Barnabas suffers in similar uncertainty. 'Is it actually castle service that Barnabas does . . .', asks Olga, 'certainly he goes into offices, but are these offices the real Castle? And even if the Castle does have offices, are they the offices that Barnabas is allowed to enter?' The underworld inhabited by Barnabas and K does not answer such questions.

### The realm of significance

The epistemological crisis shapes modernist notions of the transcendence of alienation. Romantics understood transcendence above all as some cultural, intellectual or emotional act which would afford a new understanding of self and of world. Thus, according to Hegel, for example, evolutionary *Geist* was realising itself in the human spirit, and human spirit would therefore eventually realise itself in this higher Principle, in relation to which it had existed hitherto only in a state of mutual estrangement.

Such epistemology is as profoundly optimistic as is all else that is truly romantic. Hegel's Marxist disciples retained this optimism; but Kierkegaard and all true modernists did not. Kierkegaard's concept of the 'leap of faith', for instance, assumes that he who has faith nevertheless persists in a state of absolute uncertainty dependent upon the 'absurdity' of divine grace, and that his faith thus remains incomprehensible to the faithful and to all other men.

Epistemological crisis is indeed central to modernism, as Kafka's work shows. Like Lewis, Kafka reinterpreted the antithesis of alienated and transcendental conditions as an antithesis of the realm of life—where men merely lived—and the realm of significance—where they knew their own existence. But that the many endure only an unconscious life is for Kafka, as for Kierkegaard, simply a single phase of the epistemological crisis. For even the one either cannot, or is extremely unlikely to, enter the realm of significance; and although a man might gain the realm of significance, might know himself for what he is, here too he seems to be beset by uncertainty.

Nevertheless Kafka does recognise a dichotomy between 'life', in which unmitigated incomprehension reigns, and 'significance' ('art' may be too strong a word) where, if incomprehension continues, it is at least known to continue, and where life might be some day understood, if only in part. The realm of life, the experience of the many, is the realm which obtains merely as life, as the materialism, the greed and the lust upon which is established the blind pettiness of the philistine regime. The realm of significance is the realm where all these things still obtain, but where there is some approximation to comprehension, however slight.

America offered Kafka both the subject for an elaborate critique of life in the urban world and also a suitable symbol of the realm of significance: a New World which—though in a sense transcendental—is still quite mundane in its reproduction or repetition of the Old World that is the realm of mere life. For the realm of significance *is* the realm of life, because life's significance is life itself.

'Once', wrote Kafka in 1911, 'I planned a novel, in which two brothers fought each other, one of whom went to America, while the other stayed in a European prison.' That the 'European prison' of the realm of life may even be preferable to the 'American' realm of significance, is shown in *America* where the Statue of Liberty holds aloft not a torch of illumination but a sword of judgement or destruction.

If Kafka's America is no romantic transcendental state, nor is the Nature Theatre of Oklahoma which recruits Karl Rossmann as a member. 'Join us if you want to be an artist!' announces this mysterious organisation, which advertises itself with devils and angels as 'the greatest theatre in the world'. Karl Rossmann does want to be an artist, and is acclaimed as such. But he discovers that to be an artist in the Nature Theatre seems to mean, for him at least, to be 'Negro, a factory worker', whose name and status specify the servitude exacted by the urban world.

In *The Trial* the realm of significance is much more closely connected with the realm of life than is 'America' with 'Europe' in Kafka's first novel. The court and Josef K's bank are almost one: the court employing bank staff about its business, and even executing punishments on the bank's premises. But the court, though almost identical with the bank, remains a different order. The court-bank, considered simply as financial institution, is mere life; but, considered as the vehicle of the transcendental law, it bears the significance of existence.

*The Castle*'s theme, it would appear, is K's struggle to get into the castle. But, throughout the work, he is in the village and he learns on the novel's very first page that whoever lives in the village 'lives so to speak in the castle itself.' Yet the castle remains the sphere in which life is at last known, if only in its unintelligibility. When K returns to the village from the slopes beneath the castle, 'a great bell' rings merrily above him only to fall silent as 'a feeble monotonous little bell' begins to sound, 'perhaps from above, perhaps right in the village.' The 'little bell' of mere life must be in the village—even though, so to speak, that is the castle— because only the castle—even though, so to speak, that is the village—affords the 'great bell' of meaning.

Many criticis have interpreted Kafka's work precisely as a search for meaning, or identity. They
envisage that search as the pursuit of some good some-
where, the quest, for example, of an existential realisa-
tion of self which all of us would choose if only we
knew that choice was open to us. Kafka, it is argued,
seeks a meaning to the life of modern man; and all
men, it is assumed, would desire that meaning as the
highest good. But this interpretation minimises the
degree to which a modernist like Kafka makes
the transcendental into the descendental.

Kafka may posit a realm of significance which constitutes an existence higher or at least other than mere
life. But the significance does remain the significance
of life, and life is, on the modernist analysis, calamitous. Kafka described his work as a 'descent to the
dark powers', as 'the service of the devil', and he
expressed the darkness of the realm of significance in
the physical darkness which pervades his fiction.

As Karl Rossmann leaves senator Jacob for the
worse disasters that await him, his uncle was 'hard to
recognise in the twilight of his room'; when K leaves
the inn after accepting the humiliating office of school
caretaker, 'it was undoubtedly already beginning to
get dark'; and while the priest tells Josef K the parable
of the law, 'It was dreary day no more but indeed the
dead of night.' In this darkness it can at last be seen
how darkened is life, and how obscure is the true self
of man.

In this darkness, too, both K and Josef K are seen
to realise within themselves all the world's corruption.

Thus Josef K, while seeming to denounce the court, becomes a worthy official of that institution, who dreams of salvation through the court, and who punishes an accused man in the offices of the court, and his own warders in a lumber room of the bank. The existential identity so revealed—if not to Josef K himself—is plainly descendental. 'We are drowning in filth!' he exclaims.

Filth though it may be, the descendental realm of significance draws to it the one, whose task is nothing else than to quit the realm of the many for the sphere of understanding. The warders tell Josef K that the law seeks out the guilty, but *The Trial* shows that the guilty—if Josef K be such—seek out the law. For like the other accused men, he neglects his business; seeks to attend the court when it is not sitting; and is inspired to divine the password without which, it seems, none can enter the interrogation chamber.

From the realm of significance the philistine many are to be excluded. Perhaps Kafka's esotericism is best illustrated by his demand that, after his death, his work should be burnt. Yet that it would not be burnt is a possibility on which Kafka must have reckoned, and against which he prepared those strictly literary devices that make his writings so opaque.

Kafka boasted of the 'great expense of art' which enabled him to make of his fiction 'a game in secret'. Even as published, his works give ample evidence of his tendency to conceal his intentions and protect his doctrines from philistine eyes. Many of his more or less finished pieces seem still to defeat all attempts to determine the significance to which their ominous and mysterious air lays claim. The major works add symbol to symbol and allusion to allusion so thoroughly and so carefully that, in the words of his English translator, 'countless meanings' can be found in what Kafka has written. Thus, though the evident density and obscurity of Kierkegaard's writing finds no parallel in the apparent clarity of Kafka's prose, the esoteric cause is at least as well served by the latter as by the former.

Esoteric method is designed to keep from the many the transcendental doctrine whose vulgarisation can only reinforce the alienated condition of man. This purpose is illustrated in Kafka's 'parable of the law'. According to the parable, a 'man from the country' is, from moment to moment, denied entrance to the door of the law until, as he dies, the doorkeeper declares that the door, which he is about to close, has been kept open for the man from the country alone.

The parable's fundamental esotericism lies in the deceitfulness of the doorkeeper's last words. For the unsuccessful applicant can be associated, as critics have observed, with the agrarian peoples of post-exilic Judaism, who were known to the orthodox as men or people 'of the country'. The people of the country were excluded from the esoteric system of Temple worship, partly because they handled animals—and hence were unclean—and partly because their remoteness from the Temple denied them the opportunity to observe the necessary ritual purifications. The 'man from the country' of the parable is, so identified, the vulgar many who are to be excluded from the truth. He is indeed—to change the metaphor—the philistine to whom the significance of existence is refused.

## Genius as victim

The transcendental personality which proves itself equal to the modernist condition of transcendence must display remarkable greatness, at least of fortitude; and such greatness is to be found in Kierkegaard's concept of existential genius and even in the constructs of Lewis's satire, such as the characters of Tarr or Kell-Imrie.

Kafka presents an altogether different picture, however. His fiction, reeking of the grandest and most portentous fate in every allusive word, is a setting from which the figures which appear within it derive an odour of the highest destiny. In this fiction, the very stones cry out to acclaim the greatness of the transcendental. But Kafka denies his characters the great human powers usually associated with genius, and especially with heroic genius, and has weighed them down with manifold imperfections.

Men like Georg Bendemann, Gregor Sama or Josef K are wretched urbanites whose mediocrity seems to resist even the greatness of their disastrous end. The heroine of Kafka's late story 'Josephine the Singer' is an artist and does reach for the highest garlands: but she is only a mouse and her singing is a mere whistling noise. The hero of 'A Hunger Artist' is a man who makes prodigious public fasts and eventually kills himself; yet, as he dies, he confesses that he achieved his great feats only 'because I could not find any food I liked. Had I found it, believe me, I would have caused no sensation but would have stuffed myself like you and all the rest'.

Kafka's characters would lack the great human qualities of genius if Kafka, following Kierkegaard's example, had located genius outside his work. Some of Kierkegaard's writings, such as *Repetition*, use the concept of the 'true reader', the one for whom the esoteric transcendental doctrine is prepared. Kafka's esoteric fiction also seems to presuppose a true reader: the writer himself perhaps, or the little circle to which he read his work. For the fiction continually raises the question why, in so great if so dark a world, no great deeds are done and no great men appear; and it may be that this question can be correctly answered only by the one who understands and accepts the doctrine that generates the fiction, namely, the true reader. In short, the concept of the true reader, genius taken decisively out of art and established if precariously in life, might explain the undeniable mediocrity, the apparent philistinism, of Kafka's characters.

But that genius is to be found among these characters and not simply in the concept of the true reader, can be argued from the assumptions of the traditional romantic idea of genius. According to this idea, genius can exist—in the condition of alienation—only in an alienated state, and must endure an alienated consciousness. In other words, while alienation persists, the many enter even into the one, who becomes truly and purely one only when alienation is transcended.

Kafka's 'Letter to his Father' attributes such an alienated consciousness to himself. Kafka here complains that he has inherited from his father's side, from the Kafkas, the philistine drive to business and to life, that is, to the affairs of the urban world: and only from his mother's side, from the priestly Löwys, those higher drives which work secretly to other ends.

The higher drives are also present in Kafka's characters. Both Josef K and K desire the transcendental, or the descendental, as the one alone can, and the unmixed philistine cannot. Josef K and K do demonstrate much more of the philistine than do, say, Medardus or Kreisler; but that is no more than the measure of modernist pessimism. For a modernist thinks the outcome of genius's struggle a good deal less certain than it is in the work of a romantic such as Hoffmann.

And what awaits genius in the descendental state of modernist theory is much less attractive than what greets him in the transcendental state of romantic theory. 'At least for a moment' the castle's great bell made K's 'heart tremble, as if it threatened him—so painful indeed was the sound—with the fulfilment of what he vaguely desired.' The great bell tells K what the transcendental is, and its tones are like the voice of a castle official. For should such an official answer a call to the castle (which is impossible) it would be better to 'flee from the telephone before the first sound is heard.' The transcendental is the realm of significance, and that must be a realm of suffering because the significance of life is suffering

Indeed Kafka interpreted alienation as suffering which could alone be transcended through an understanding, if only of the incomprehensibility, of suffering. The neurasthenia which Kafka feared, and the tuberculosis which killed him, realised such mortification in his own life. Kafka's scheme for an ascetic guild of workmen who would live in poverty and chastity indicates his belief that the good life—that is perhaps, in modernist terms, the bad life—must be a life of voluntary suffering. Kafka's characters, and above all those characters which approximate most closely to the one, are required to share, to live out, this belief.

Alienation's austere significance is finally realised in death. Brod recalls that K was to die in the village; and many other Kafka characters die before the reader's eyes: by drowning like Georg Bendemann; by stabbing like Josef K; by starving like the hunger artist; through injury like Gregor Samsa; or after twelve hours of torture like the commandant of 'In the Penal Colony'.

Yet sickness too represents transcendental suffering. Kafka's early works attribute sickness to transcendental personality itself. In 'The Urban World' Franz, the true son who belongs to the higher realm, is a 'feeble man', unlike Oscar, the false son who belongs to the world of the many; and the 'yellow complexion' of Georg Bendemann's friend, the true son of 'The Judgement', 'seemed to indicate a hidden disease.'

Kafka's concern with disease enables him to make much of beds, which occur frequently throughout his work. The ambiguous symbol of the bed—retreat of the sick, but pleasure ground of the lustful—exploits the Freudian concept of sexuality as the torment of an animalism inseparable from illness. Such suffering may even be the most ubiquitous of all those austerities endured by Kafka's characters. Yet Kafka did not wish to separate the transcendental abnegation that arises out of the urban world from that which arises out of the sexual underworld. Karl Rossmann's travels, for example, therefore make a tale both of sexual calamities and of social and economic degradation. The son of a respectable bourgeois European family, Karl hopes to be an engineer or even a pianist, but becomes instead an impoverished emigrant to America where he works first as lift boy, then as servant and finally, it seems, as a labourer.

Suffering might be thought to be martyrdom in a work such as 'The Judgement', where the Russian priest quells the mob by displaying 'a broad cross of blood cut in the palm of his hand'; and where the maid servant acclaims the moribund Georg Bendemann as 'Jesus'. Both the priest's self-mortification and Georg's suicide represent—at least to the true reader and perhaps also to themselves—the ascetic character of the transcendental: and to represent this truth is an achievement which might make mere suffering into martyrdom.

Yet, in the last resort, martyrdom is an idea foreign to the phase of European culture in which Kafka

appears, not only because the transcendental has become the descendental, but because even the descendental seems unlikely to be achieved. Thus when
Josef K succumbs to the fetid atmosphere of the court
offices, bystanders expect to see in him 'some great
transformation', but they are disappointed because—
in such a world as this—Josef K is simply the victim
who must 'die like a dog'.

In Kafka, and especially in *The Trial*, genius has
ceased to be martyr and appears merely as victim in
the wretched mediocrity of his alleged criminality.
For great forces are turned against the one, who is
crushed between the horrors of alienation and the
terrifying self-knowledge in which alone, according to
modernists, those horrors may be transcended. Genius
continues—if in disguise—and the sufferings of martyrdom are intensified. But nothing, it seems, is achieved.
There is 'Plenty of hope—for God—' said Kafka, 'no
end of hope—only not for us.'

# 6

BECKETT'S TRANSCENDENTAL NIHILISM

## *The World of Habit*

THOSE who live in Kafka's world without hope are, Beckett observes, 'victims and prisoners'. But in this world 'a compromise' is 'effected between the individual and his environment' which does enable him to exist (if not exactly as a human being); and that compromise is habit. 'Life is habit. Or rather life is a succession of habits', Beckett concludes.

Through habit existence is conveniently transformed into repetitive trivialities such as are invented by Beckett's characters, who count steps, arrange biscuits, sort pebbles, or indulge in the permutations that while away so much of Beckett's novel *Watt*. 'We always did find something, eh Didi, to give us the impression we exist', says Estragon to Vladimir in *Waiting for Godot*. What results is of course a philistine, an imitation man, but a man precisely suited to our world.

Beckett criticises even the highest achievements of that world, as can be seen for example in his severe critique of art. At different periods Beckett has condemned most phases of art. His earliest publications, like the contemporary work of Lewis, deride romanticism, and especially romantic transcendentalism. The 'button-busting' Smeraldina, who figures in *More Pricks than Kicks* and elsewhere, quotes Goethe, plays Beethoven and personifies 'the most iniquitous excesses of a certain kind of sublimation': namely, the musical-erotic paradise. So does Celia, the prostitute-heroine of *Murphy*, who takes her name from the patron saint of music and lives on sex. Murphy opposes the doctrine represented by this champion of voluptuous romanticism with all the dry zeal of his fellow neo-classicists. Indeed, Murphy remains 'unromantic to the last', if only in pun, because his death is 'a classical case of misadventure'.

In later years Beckett began to identify sensual materialism no longer with the romantic but with the classical. Beckett's *Three Dialogues* with Georges Duthuit insist 'that art has always been bourgeois', and isolate within this philistine tradition especially the art of the renaissance. 'Italian painters', Beckett declares, 'surveyed the world with the eyes of building contractors' and 'never stirred from the field of the possible'.

In 1961 Beckett gave an interview in which he dissociated his aesthetic principles from those embodied in the church of the Madeleine in Paris, whose 'classical lines' were meant to evoke 'the Age of Reason'. 'This is clear', Beckett was reported to have said. 'This does not allow the mystery to invade us. With classical art, all is settled.' The classical has now become the habitual, the mechanical and the philistine.

Yet Beckett's position may not have changed. For he intends, both early and late, to criticise the philistine wherever it may be found; and it may be found in the romantic and the classical, which are, as degraded by a world of habit, indivisible. Thus *More Pricks than*

*Kicks* ends with the 'classico-romantic working man' who 'sang a little song . . . drank his bottle of stout . . . dashed away a tear' and 'made himself comfortable'. 'So', the book concludes, 'it goes in the world.'

Habitual materialism of culture parallels the mechanical acquisitiveness of economic life. Gross love of property is fully represented in Beckett's work, where derelicts like Molloy or Malone are as committed to their few belongings as is the respectable bourgeois Moran to his jars of lager, his resilient Wilton and his aromatic lemon verbena. From this lust for possession springs production, and hence employment and the rigid social roles, exacted by employment, that comprise what in *Murphy* is called the 'mercantile gehenna'.

*Molloy* expands the system of employment into a 'vast organisation', forensic or judicial in character, like the 'great organisation' of the law in *The Trial*. The chief of this vast organisation is Youdi, below whom are messengers such as Gaber and, below them, agents like Moran, who must force their children to share their toil. The system employs not merely the physical body but existence itself, which it alienates into new and perhaps permanently dehumanised forms. Thus, in the world of *Happy Days*—from which employment has apparently long disappeared—one quarter of the utterances of the wretched Willie are reports of situations vacant.

Employment rests upon the habitual roles of master and servant, each of which categories alienates the other (and thus man) into a limited, subhuman being. Beckett's accounts of jobs—or indeed of families,

173

hospitals and asylums—draw much of their strength from these archetypes, whom Beckett interprets as keeper and kept, tormentor and victim. Such relationships provide the many with masks of identity which seem to organise, in a fashion acceptable at least to themselves, the fragmented reality of their existence. Individuals are therefore yoked together, rather than united with each other, just as Jacques Moran is roped to his father in *Molloy*, and Lucky is roped to his master Pozzo in *Waiting for Godot*.

Though the rigidity of the philistine order preserves the social world (if at the price of dehumanising it), forces active in each member of that world hold individuals down to an animal level. Beckett finds disgust inseparable from life and its material conditions. His characters urinate, crepitate, defecate and vomit in quantities, and with a frequency, uncommon even in modern fiction, although they rarely belch. As animals, men must always suffer. Pus is prominently mentioned in Beckett's work; and sores, chiefly on the head or legs, are commonly met with. Skin diseases, such as impetigo, eczema and psoriasis, afflict major and minor figures alike.

Animality rests upon the sexual process, without which animal existence would cease. Hence sexuality forms an important subject of Beckett's critique of the condition of alienation. Sexual satisfaction is an abomination, fittingly if vainly pursued by the decrepit, whose condition excludes the deceptively idyllic, and emphasises the repugnantly insane elements of sexuality. It is therefore with a certain disdain that *More*

*Pricks than Kicks* describes the passion of the aged cretin Jimmy the Duck Skyrm for the lame and ancient nymphomaniac Hermione Nautzsche.

Though vile, sex is a habit that the many will not do without. Mrs Rooney in *All that Fall* demands 'fifty years of twice daily love like a Paris horsebutcher's regular'. Mindful of Nell Gwynn's reputation, not to speak of Eskimo Nell, Beckett creates a series of Nellies, from Miss Rosie Dew's dachshund on heat, the 'hot dog' that disrupts Murphy's contemplations, to the Nell of *Endgame* with her opening line, 'What is it, my pet? Time for love?'

Most of Beckett's work indicates that the persistence of sexuality is—on the whole—the work of woman who, as in Lewis or in Kafka, comes to personify the lower order, not only because she is held to contain the mechanical principle of sex, but because she is the guardian of the habitual round of worldly normality. That normality excludes a transcendental sexuality. Women, complains Murphy, 'can't love for five minutes without wanting it abolished in brats and house bloody wifery.'

This joke must not obscure the deadliness of the female. It is, after all, Celia's passion for estranging normality that forces Murphy into work, and so leads to his death at work. The sexual world, that is, the habitual world, is indeed a world of death. Thus Estragon thinks the Dead Sea a nice place for a honeymoon; and Schubert's 'Death and the Maiden' is the accompaniment to *All that Fall*.

Bergson regarded the deadened man of the present

order as one in whom rigid matter triumphed over enfeebled *élan vital*. Lewis embodies this notion in the symbol of the cripple, a procedure which Beckett re-uses with a rigidity worthy of matter. We learn from *More Pricks than Kicks* that Belacqua's feet are in ruins; and so it goes on in Beckett's later works: Watt is often stiff-legged; Moran is lamed; and Molloy is reduced to crawling, like Worm—the invention of the legless Unnamable—and like the narrator of *How It Is*. Cooper in *Murphy* and Clov in *Endgame* suffer acathisia, which prevents them from sitting; and Miss Rosie Dew endures panpygoptosis, 'a distressing patho-logical condition in which the thighs are suppressed'.

Beckett also symbolises Bergsonian inelasticity in the bicycle, the machine of transport with which Molloy and Moran transport their mechanical selves. But more recent Beckett characters are confined to con-tainers: the Unnamable to his jar, Nag and Nell to dustbins, Winnie to her mound, and the cast of *Play* to urns of carefully prescribed dimensions. The uni-formity and rigidity of such fundamentally *characterless* figures serves to display the nature of a humanity which is sustained only by the mechanisms of habit.

### The failure of knowledge

Beckett's *Proust* concludes with an enthusiastic sum-mary of the concept of transcendental music: 'the ideal and immaterial statement of the essence of a unique beauty, a unique world' that 'damns the life of the body on earth as a pensum.' That beauty is, however, inaccessible to a critic of romanticism, such as Beckett, for whom the modernist tradition has closely defined the transcendental (or rather the descendental) as a realm of significance which affords, at its best and highest, simply knowledge of the calamity which is the realm of mere life.

The two realms are fundamental to Beckett's writings, and especially to *Watt*. The novel's first and last pages reveal life lived by what now pass for men, the ludicrous inhabitants of the animal kingdom of '*Diana's blushing bud*'; and the sufferings of this realm are exemplified by Mr Hackett's childhood injury and deformity. But the centre of the book reveals to us what might seem to be the temple of a God, who 'neither comes nor goes' but 'seems to abide in his place' where his servants or devotees 'rest a little while in his branches'. In that temple life's meaning might perhaps be revealed. Yet the temple is the house of one called by the ominous negative *Knott*; and the creed to be associated with Mr Knott's house seems to be the impossibility of knowing anything.

Beckett often uses the example of Descartes to illustrate that incompetence of cognition which seems to put the realm of significance quite beyond reach. In explaining and justifying rational scientific enquiry, Descartes asserted that mind and body were separate. Because the mind was distinct from the body, it could know the body (just as it could know the world outside the body) as an external object susceptible to rational investigation.

Mind knew both body and world through reason, which a perfect God had equipped with innate ideas that—because they issued from the divine perfection—must be perfectly true. So long as mind was thought to enjoy this God-given endowment, and to use it upon the objects of cognition, mind and body, self and world, remained in unity with each other. But the entire system rested upon the divine being, about which modern man, like Beckett's characters, has come to entertain the most profound doubts. 'The bastard! He doesn't exist!' exclaims Hamm at the conclusion of his futile prayers in *Endgame*: and if God does not exist, nor does the omnipotent Cartesian mind established upon the divine gift of innate ideas.

The mind's admired independence then becomes solitude, weakness and helplessness. Descartes' disciple Geulincx had conceived mind as the lordly sojourner within the body, as free as the passenger who can even, if he choose, walk east along the deck of a westbound ship. But to Molloy, the mind seems merely 'a sadly rejoicing slave' that crawls eastwards 'on the black boat of Ulysses' to gaze helplessly upon the 'futile wake'.

Like Lewis, Beckett also points to the evidences of epistemological disorders afforded by the work of Bergson; and he has found in *Remembrance of Things Past* a highly appropriate text for a Bergsonian disquisition on the alienated world. 'The individual', claims Beckett, 'is the seat of a constant process of decantation, decantation from the vessel containing the fluid of future time, sluggish, pale and monochrome, to the vessel containing past time, agitated and multicoloured by the phenomena of its hours.' The individual is really, therefore, 'a succession of individuals', a series of Lewisian time-slices, 'whose permanent reality, if any, can only be apprehended as a retrospective hypothesis.'

Individuals can therefore know neither themselves nor, *a fortiori*, other men. For every human being is a 'series of events' which cannot coincide with any other because each occurs within different temporal continua. 'When it is a case of human intercourse', writes Beckett in *Proust*, 'we are faced by the problem of an object whose mobility is not merely a function of the subject's, but independent and personal: two separate and immanent dynamisms related by no system of synchronisation.' In Proust's novel, for example, Marcel can only secure for himself that Albertine who develops from the Albertine that he loved and set out to win.

The realm of significance seems to be lost, for subject and object are divided, and Beckett appears to reject any positivist solution to this problem. Positivism proposes to reunite subject and object by excluding metaphysical speculation, and by using only elementary propositions, which, it is hoped, will match the elementary facts of empirical cognition and communication. Watt is positivist man who says of a pot 'Pot, pot', but finds to his dismay that the pot remains only 'almost a pot', by the hair's breadth which destroys positivist certainty. In Mr Knott's house, objects 'vanish in the farce of their properties'; and these properties, though perceptible only in temporary combinations of variables, together constitute the solid, resistant immensity of matter.

Mr Knott's house is indeed a realm of epistemological problems. Just as, in *The Castle*, the 'picture' of K's employer Klamm 'varies, and perhaps not so much as Klamm's real appearance varies', so 'the figure' of Watt's employer Mr Knott 'was seldom the same figure, from one glance to the next, but so various' that Watt 'would never have supposed it was the same, if he had not known that it was Mr Knott.'

Yet despite these tribulations, Beckett's characters still manifest the marks of the one. Art is an important, and symptomatic, enterprise for these characters. Thus, in the *Molloy* trilogy, Molloy, Moran, Lemuel and the Unnamable are all writers; the hero of 'Assumption' is probably a painter; the percipient madman of *Endgame* is a painter, and so is Bram van Velde, who serves as a paradigm of transcendental art in the *Three Dialogues*.

'The Calmative' and 'Texts for Nothing' introduce heroic genius in the figure of 'one Joe Breem, or Breen', the lighthouse keeper's boy. Joe Breem's 'sheer heroism' can now provide merely the happy ending of 'a comedy, for children'. He belongs to a world lost and the narrator of 'Texts for Nothing' remarks—as he returns home by another route—'A blessing he was not waiting for me, poor old Breem, or Breen.' Yet Joe Breem is regretted rather than despised. Even as the narrator of the 'Texts' takes another road home, he confesses that his is 'the way that was not mine'.

Indeed if the narrator of the 'Texts' laments lost genius, the Unnamable claims to personify the transcendental spirit. 'I am Matthew and I am the angel', he declares, 'I who came before the cross, before the sinning, came into the world, came here.' It is true that the Unnamable has 'nothing in common' with Prometheus, who might well seem to represent heroic genius, but that is because Prometheus 'mocked the gods, invented fire, denatured clay and domesticated the horse, in a word obliged humanity.' The Unnamable, with his angelic and pre-Christian claims, and his present confinement and torment, may rather look like a superior Prometheus dedicated, not to materialist normality, but to the higher values of modernism.

Yet Beckett's idea of the transcendental personality really extends at most to the category of the martyr, and not to that of the hero. Genius could only transcend alienation through suffering, because it is suffering which, *Proust* argues, 'opens a window on the real and is the main condition of the artistic experience.'

The Christ symbol is therefore prominent in Beckett. Watt, declares Goff Nixon, 'would literally turn the other cheek, I honestly believe, if he had the energy'; and, when Watt appears with his face and hands 'bloody' and with 'thorns in his scalp', Sam reports that, 'His resemblance, at that moment to the Christ believed by Bosch, then hanging in Trafalgar Square, was so striking, that I remarked it.'

But *More Pricks than Kicks* dismisses Christ as the first in 'the series of slick suicides' that, by definition, has no place in the seriousness of a modernism for which even genius's triumph is a most austere affair. The martyr thus becomes the victim, whose improbable victory may be worse than his likely defeat.

Furthermore, Beckettian genius displays a peculiarly acute form of that alienation in which the principle of the many largely penetrates and threatens to subdue the principle of the one. Genius thus appears almost only as genius failed. Belacqua is 'not *serious*'; and that grievous charge may be set against many later Beckett characters, from the irresolute Murphy to the philistinely possessive narrator of *How It Is*.

The Beckettian victim-genius is perhaps best represented by old Mr Kelly in *Murphy*. Mr Kelly's ambition is to fly his kite—'the speck that was he'—out of sight of the mortal world. At the very end of the book, the kite has 'disappeared from view'; and the enraptured Mr Kelly believes he is about to 'measure the distance from the unseen to the seen', a suitably transcendental ambition. But while he dozes the string snaps, the kite is lost and, 'a ghastly, lamentable figure', he pursues the kite in a suicidal effort only frustrated by Celia's intervention.

### Existence and non-existence

Despite the great unlikelihood that the transcendental (or the descendental) can be achieved, given Beckett's premisses, much of his work seems to provide characteristic modernist insights into the transcendental. Beckett apparently assents to the modernist presumption that, whether the transcendental is a new view or a first view of life itself, that view shows life to be not a heaven but a hell.

Belacqua, Beckett's first hero, takes his name from a character in Dante's antepurgatorial travels; and *More Pricks than Kicks* reveals a sinister picture of what one of the book's characters calls the 'Gehenna of links'. Later works, in which Belacqua reappears from time to time, develop the concept of a hell which is life because life is hell. 'That's what hell will be like', declares Henry in *Embers*, 'small chat to the babbling of Lethe about the good old days when we wished we were dead. Price of margarine fifty years ago. And now.'

The revelation that the realm of life amounts to hell deranges those who enter the realm of significance. In *Endgame* Hamm tells of a painter who was 'appalled' by 'all that loveliness' visible through the window. 'All he had seen', says Hamm, 'was ashes.' So the painter is 'a madman', 'in the asylum', like Murphy or Watt. But theirs is an aesthetic madness, a transcendental state, quite unlike the condition of 'the other scum' who suffer a merely clinical insanity, the madness of life, so to speak rather than the madness of significance.

Murphy believes 'that nothing less than a slap-up psychosis could consummate his life's strike.' The great theme of *Murphy* is, however, that Murphy yearns for the higher aesthetic madness and not the vulgar lunacy of the inhabitants of the Magdalen Mental Mercyseat. Beckettian aesthetic madness is an 'escape' from the world of habit 'into the spacious annexe of mental alienation'. This 'rare dispensation' is, of course, torment—it is a real madness—yet it is, for those who can endure it, a higher state than alienated normality —it is a real dispensation.

The concept of transcendental madness is quite closely associated with the ladders, from this order to that, whose appearance, both in *Murphy* and in *Watt*, has provoked much scholarly discussion. Beckett has discouraged the view that these are the same sort of means of ascent as the propositions which Wittgenstein described as ladders to be thrown away once they have been climbed. But no allusion to Wittgenstein need be assumed for the ladder motif to express the notion that existence off and above the ladder is existence in the realm of significance, and therefore aesthetic madness.

There are three ladders in *Watt*. Mr Hackett falls off the first of these; but he is a denizen of the realm of mere life, of deadening normality, who simply breaks his back. Arsène falls off the second ladder but, because he is in Mr Knott's house, he discovers thereby 'the reversed metamorphosis. The laurel back into Daphne. The old thing where it always was, back again.'

Whereas Mr Hackett falls into a 'dark yard', Arsène falls into a yard full of sunlight. For the 'old thing' is revealed to Arsène in its true significance, and is not merely reconfirmed in its commonplace, habitual triviality. Unlike Mr Hackett, therefore, Arsène is not simply maimed. On the contrary, his inner being is transformed to the point where he begins to experience aesthetic madness, suspecting, for example, that the 'reversed metamorphosis' has changed the pipe in his mouth into 'an epileptic's dental wedge'.

Arsène's ascent to existence off the ladder occurs, or seems to occur, when 'a tiny little thing' slips in the great mound of habitual life. Another 'tiny little thing'—failure to name the pot—frees Watt from the mechanical positivism which is the third ladder of the novel. Mr Hackett's hunch denies him the material 'foothills' which, as a cripple, he cannot climb. But the intellectual or spiritual trauma which Watt suffers when he abandons his ladder leaves him 'in the hollow, at the foot of all the hills at last, the ways down, the ways up, and free, free at last. . . .' This is Watt's transcendental liberty, a liberty directly contrasted with Mr Hackett's physical constraint. Yet this transcendental liberty is the madness that consigns Watt, bloodied and at first unintelligible, to the asylum.

Beckett's concept of the transcendental is not exhausted by the notion that existence is found to signify hell or madness. On the contrary, Beckett develops a further, extreme doctrine, which may be termed transcendental nihilism, and which seems to owe at least something to Schopenhauer.

Schopenhauer argued that mind could only transcend the estranging effects of will, and especially of will to live, by rising to a non-existence, to a 'nothing' or a nirvana. Furthermore, he reasoned that this transcendental nothing stood to will and its domain much as the realm of significance stood to the realm of life. Certainly, he admitted, he taught only a higher nothing, but then life was simply a lower nothing. Thus the first volume of *The World as Will and Representation* ends with these words: 'We freely acknowledge that what remains after the complete abolition of the will is indeed nothing, for all who are still full of the will. But conversely, to those in whom the will has turned and denied itself, this very real world of ours with all its suns and galaxies, is—nothing.'

The idea that the transcendental significance of existence is non-existence, dominates Beckett's work. Nothingness, together with the faculty of exultation, is the transcendental state demanded by the Unnamable, who dreams of 'the blissful knowledge that you are nobody for all eternity.' The narrator of *How It Is*, afflicted by his habitual itch for property and subjectivity, still believes that 'they'd be good moments in the dark and mud hearing nothing saying nothing capable of nothing nothing.'

Transcendental non-existence is a state more easily described than achieved, though even description must remain exceedingly elusive. Transcendental nothing might be thought to require an erasure of conscious self: Watt, for instance, declares—as he loses consciousness—'Now I am at liberty . . . I am free to come and go as I please.' On the other hand, it might be thought that the transcendental nullity demands not man, conscious or unconscious, but the removal of man altogether. Beckett's characters embrace this possibility when they seek a chaos of fragments whose substantive non-existence signifies and hence, in modernist terms, transcends the non-existence in which man is estranged. 'Oh to be in atoms, in atoms! ATOMS!' exclaims Mrs Rooney.

Beckett has chosen to represent non-existence chiefly by the idea of life in the womb, or by symbols closely related to that idea. Hats are peculiarly important to his characters, because they awake poignant memories of the caul. The padded cell, or the padded cab of 'The Expelled', also suggests the womb. Bed—where Malone lives, Moran thinks, and Mrs Rooney wants to waste away—is another uterine symbol. Yet bed is a symbol which, in Beckett's work, as the case of Mrs Rooney indicates, identifies the womb as negation of, and not preparation for, life.

This can be seen too from Beckett's use of boat symbolism. Boats are very common in Beckett, from the rowing boat in which, 'far from land', Watt 'suddenly smelt flowering currant', to the vessel with which, in *Cascando*, Woburn goes 'out to sea . . . heading nowhere', far from the 'lights . . . of the land.' And all these womb-like vehicles are carriages of death: the narrator of 'The End', for example, turns his boat into a coffin, floats out to sea, drugs himself and drowns just as, in the last moment of consciousness, he perceives the significance of 'the likeness of my life'.

Flowering currant notwithstanding, the non-existence symbolised by the uterine boat-death is no romantic paradise. Peggy Guggenheim claimed that

Beckett's 'terrible memory of life in his mother's womb' gave him 'awful crises, when he felt he was suffocating'—and suffocation is the reality of death by drowning. Non-existence is not a calm and contemplative nirvana but the terrible ascetic descendentalism which, in the modernist view, alone can overcome the present order.

Non-existence is, then, closely associated at least with death if not with madness. Hamm's exclamation, 'Put me in my coffin!' expresses the suicidal tendency of many Beckett characters, for whom (drowning apart) death by gas seems the most suitable end: as the Hindu polyhistor who, in *Murphy*, puts his head in the oven, admits. For gas is etymologically 'chaos and chaos gas'. Gas, the meaningless oscillation of atoms, which embodies Beckett's transcendental nihilism, appropriately abolishes Murphy, by explosion, and Belacqua, by poisoning.

But suicide's benefits do not adequately express those elements in modernism which seek absolutely to transcend the mankind of the many. Murder begins in Beckett with McCabe, the assassin of *More Pricks than Kicks*, and involves various other figures in his work, including Molloy, Moran and Lemuel. *Malone Dies* notes that Macmann desired 'to make a clean sweep and have nothing before his eyes but a patch of brown earth rid of its parasites'; and Clov declares, 'I love order. It's my dream. A world where all would be silent and still and each thing in its last place, under the last dust.'

## *Nihilism and non-expression*

Beckett seeks to develop his transcendental nihilism by drawing upon a tradition of aesthetics which distinguishes a sphere of utility, of material interest and habit, from the sphere of inutility to which art belongs, because art precisely does not arise from material interest and habit. Such aesthetics holds art to be useless, because it is above the expedience of the alienated condition, and because it reaches out to that higher realm of unity and perfection in which the merely utilitarian has no part. Furthermore, because morality is no more than a particular calculus of interests, or a particular regime of worldly organisation, art is held to be amoral or, if it be preferred, immoral.

In practice art retains some substance or content, and this residuum always threatens to degrade what should be the transcendental into a mundane work of utility or morality: into the didactic, for example, or the pornographic. Form or style seems the most reliably aesthetic—and hence transcendental—element of art, and substance or content the dispensable, mundane element of art. Hence transcendental aesthetics tends always to exalt form and to minimise content.

Romantic criticism identified sculpture (a mass of substance slightly chipped by form) and literature (the narration of thoughts and deeds profoundly substantive) as inferior arts. Music—at its most earthly a system of sounds, each of which was in any event soon over—seemed to romantic critics the highest of all arts, if not the only art properly so defined by the criteria of transcendental aesthetics: and such is the doctrine which appears at the end of Beckett's *Proust*.

Music's claims stimulated the ambitions of writers who, perhaps simply because they were not musicians, hoped to show that literature could be no less musical, that is, no less formal and free of mundane content, than music itself. A novel about nothing became the ideal of great literary formalists who sought thus to create a transcendental structure unmarred by the things of earth. Beckett has evolved these ideas still further. He proposes an art which involves 'The expression that there is nothing to express, nothing with which to express, nothing from which to express, no power to express, no desire to express, together with the obligation to express.'

The 'nothing to express', which the artist is mysteriously obliged to express, might be the lower nothing, the void within the realm of mere life, or the higher nothing, the non-existence towards which transcendental nihilism strives. That this nothing is the higher nothing is shown by Beckett's claim that what he calls 'occasion' or 'aliment'—that is, the mundane content condemned by transcendental aesthetics—is to be eliminated from such art.

This seems to be an exceedingly difficult task, because elimination of occasion may be simply another occasion: and Beckett admits to have no answer to this objection. Indeed, as expositor and practitioner of his own aesthetic theory, if such he be, Beckett seems to accept occasions theoretically as solid as the 'fruits on plates' that the *Three Dialogues* deplore.

For Beckett is reported as saying in 1956 that, 'I'm working with impotence, ignorance'; while in 1961 he is stated to have said that, 'To find a form that accommodates the mess, that is the task of the artist now.' Since impotence, ignorance and mess—especially mess distinguished from, because accommodated by, form—do seem to be occasions, it could be concluded that, in this respect, Beckett diverges from his own doctrine of non-expression.

Beckett's position on the issue of form—of art, in this sense—is as ambiguous as his attitude to the problem of occasion. His *theory* appears to exclude not only occasion but art itself. Beckett says, for example, that the 'coloured plane' painted by Bram van Velde, the *Three Dialogues'* exemplar of non-expression, 'seems to have nothing to do with art', which, according to the *Dialogues*, is a 'bourgeois' activity typical of the possessive world of habit. It might be concluded therefore that Beckett seeks not art but an absolute aesthetic whose non-existence and non-expression exclude it from the sphere of art, that is, of form.

But even the product of van Velde's aesthetic activity has its plane form, not to speak of its colour; in 1961 Beckett himself explicitly counselled a search for form; and his own intensely technical writings are replete with form. Beckett seems, therefore, to fail his own theory, since both his work and his thought appear to be bound by art, as well as occasion.

But the *Three Dialogues* attribute achievement of

nihilist non-expression not to Bram van Velde, but to
the idea of van Velde that arises from Beckett's 'fancy',
and than which the van Velde of mere life is 'more
than likely', Beckett agrees, 'quite otherwise'. It is the
*idea* of van Velde where transcendental nihilism is to
be found; while Beckett's own work stands to non-
existence and non-expression as Kierkegaard's work
stands to existential faith, or perhaps as Kafka's work
stands to the realms of significance approached through
art. In other words, Beckett points the way, but the
destination belongs to the true reader, a person,
theoretically speaking, of the same type as the idea
of Bram van Velde.

Beckett's works are held progressively to abandon
the bourgeois art of the world of habit for transcendental non-expression. But there is much of mere life
even in the most non-existent of these works; and,
while that element of life may be held to contradict
the transcendental, it can be and is used to teach a
transcendental doctrine which would remain untaught
in the absolute non-expressive silence which Beckett's
characters claim to desire but usually repudiate. Even
modernism, and even Beckett, apparently continue to
call out from among the many the one who shall
transcend man's alienated condition.

Beckett's popularity, and especially the fame and
scandal of his plays, continually threatens to negate
this call by stimulating an ever-responsive philistinism.
But his work is protected from the many by an esoteric
system that reveals itself, for example, in the implicit
offence and obscurity of all his plays, or in the open

insults offered to the auditorium especially in *Waiting for Godot* and *Endgame*.

Access to the work is hindered by its defences against the many. Many of Beckett's texts maintain a double existence in English and French variants, translated or at least approved by their author. One work, *More Pricks than Kicks*, was kept from print (except for an edition of one hundred typescript copies) for nearly four decades. Other works, such as *Mercier and Camier*, have existed for a quarter of a century or more only in manuscript consulted by certain scholars. Fragments or descriptions of some texts apparently still unpublished are all that have been allowed to the public outside a small circle. What is published displays an often impenetrable brilliance of style decorated with recondite allusions and a vocabulary of remote technical terms, nonce words, and verbal rarities. 'Let him understand who can', the 'Texts for Nothing' conclude, and that man, it seems, is the one.

# 7

## THE IDEOLOGY OF GENIUS

### *From romanticism to modernism*

THOUGH most of the ideas here discussed have been used for purposes peculiar to particular persons or periods, few belong solely to the writers or the epoch examined in this book. Modern culture has a monopoly of none of these notions, and least of all the concept of the one and the many, the great sustaining archetype from which the ideology of genius derives.

These ideas can therefore scarcely be attributed to a single source. Yet the Judaeo-Christian religious tradition must commend itself to our attention as the chief medium through which our culture has received the ideas about unity and multiplicity which shape our interpretation of the phenomena of alienation. For that tradition teaches a unitary God who has made a manifold creation, now in rebellion against him.

Perhaps because of these notions' religious provenance, we often use the idea of the one and the many to make moral or even theological distinctions. We tend to think that the world is primarily, or in principle, one and that, as such, it constitutes a good or a higher existence; and we tend to fear that the world is now, or in actuality, manifold and that, as such, it constitutes a bad or a lower existence. And that moral presumption—if largely dependent simply upon a specific religious tradition—seems natural enough, since most of us egoistically perceive our self as a good or higher unitary existence located among a multiplicity of bad or lower existences, such as our worse selves or other human beings.

The psychology of perception continues so to vitalise the concept of the one and the many, even while the religious era which developed that concept yields to a secular era. But the concept of the one and the many does change during the transition from religious to secular era. In the religious era it is God and, in the secular era, it is man who is deemed to have made a multiplicity now foreign and hostile to him, and who must transcend this manifold alienation, as saviour, redeemer or genius. Marx observed that Feuerbach resolved 'the religious world into its secular basis' by revealing the 'human essence' of outwardly 'religious self-alienation'; and such too is the tendency of the entire process of secularisation.

Secular culture does more than substitute man for God. Religion indicates that men and their world are alienated and alienating, and thus identifies both as fit subjects for criticism; but religious culture must delimit its criticism upon the principle that the evil of the alienated order is bounded by God's goodness. Men and their world may be bad, but they are so—according to religion—only because they are corrupted and fallen from the divine grace which continues to obtain as a possibility for good.

But secular culture denies the existence of God and refuses to find in actual men and their world the real goodness which might be inferred of phenomena admittedly fallen but in origin the work of divine power. Hence, whereas religious culture restrains criticism by postulating a divine order above or beyond the merely phenomenal, secular culture rejects that postulate and tends always towards absolute, unlimited criticism of men and their world.

Secular culture's inability to contain evil in some determinate motive or principle intensifies this criticism. Religion not merely confined the sinful world to limits set by the over-arching sinlessness of God but also concentrated the world's sin within a particular event, such as the fall, or a particular agency, such as the devil. But secular culture repudiates the ethical synecdoche exemplified by fall and devil, and understands evil to be dispersed throughout the entire phenomenal order. In short, secular culture denies fall and devil, only to view all history as a fall and the whole world as a diabolical realm; and the more or less limited religious concept of sin is displaced by a pessimistic secular concept of unlimited evil, which underlies even the most ambitious romantic optimism.

These critical, pessimistic tendencies issue in an elaborate world critique which seeks to prove why and how men and their world are alienated into evil. That critique addresses itself to changing men and a changing world. Yet its most striking characteristic is not its flexibility, its adaptation to ever-changing subject matter, but its inflexibility, its repetition of the same basic formulas such as man made machine, the self divided, and so forth.

Change is to be seen, and new notions do appear, in the world critique. But these developments arise from within the critique itself rather than from developments in what is criticised. For the critique criticises itself, each phase of criticism becoming, in its turn, the subject matter of a new criticism which shows it to estrange men still further from true humanity.

Such criticism must stimulate efforts to reform, if not abolish, what is criticised—as it must also assume some standards (and these standards of the highest sort) by which to criticise. Both processes introduce the paradoxical necessity of something above and beyond even the most stringent criticism: a realm in which what demands criticism is indeed reformed or abolished; a criterion by which what demands criticism can indeed be criticised. In other words, absolute criticism needs the transcendental.

Furthermore, the transcendental gains from secular culture a dynamism which it lacks in religious culture. The religious transcendental realm is to be found in God and in his environment, namely, heaven. That divine realm is held—at least, by traditional Christianity—to afford a perfect and absolute satisfaction; and though some may choose not to gain that satisfaction, there is nothing problematical or uncertain about its eternal existence or its availability to those who truly desire it.

The divine realm, and the satisfaction which it offers, give religious culture a stable, even a static character. The highest that men can achieve has already been achieved by the saints who have gone

before; can still be achieved; and can never be sur-
passed. In religious culture human effort, human
aspirations, are permanently fixed and limited.

Secular culture knows no such limitations. Undoubtedly it attempts to transcend the alienation which it
discovers and describes. In fact, since men and their
world are judged more severely by secular than by
religious culture, transcendence of their imperfections
acquires even more urgency from the former than the
latter. But secular culture's critical tendencies inhibit
it from finding a single, certain and universally acknowledged realm where men's alienation, from their
best selves and from the higher values, may be transcended. Whatever is proposed as the transcendental
by one is eventually criticised by another.

In any event, the concept of a final and perfect
satisfaction has no place in secular culture which can
admit only partial satisfactions and, for this very
reason, must always be seeking new and further satisfactions. Thus secular culture is not a stable, still less a
static culture, but a highly progressive culture, continually seeking fresh goals even in the sphere of
ultimate human concerns.

Above all, secular transcendentalism contains two
special impulses to progress. Firstly, though the religious transcendental might be described as an 'infinite',
within religious culture that concept acts as an entirely
finite, if perfect, phenomenon: heaven is simply the
top storey of the three-storey universe. But the secular
transcendental is an infinite or nothing. It is the infinite
greatness after which man is ever striving. No one can

name or define that greatness: it is inexhaustible, it is infinite. Its attractive power therefore far surpasses that of the religious heaven.

Secondly, the secular transcendental lies within the sphere of man, rather than of a deity who has ceased to exist. When, for example, Lenin speaks of the 'oppressed class's really revolutionary struggle for the creation of a paradise on earth', he envisages something which—unlike the religious heaven—depends not on an external force such as divine grace, but on men's efforts alone. That is also true of all the other paradises on earth, of which secular culture has invented so many; and it is because they are paradises on earth, attainable (if at all) by man, and man only, that they have exerted such a fascination over men.

Secular transcendentalism eventually undergoes the transition from romanticism to modernism; and what emerges from this transformation is, so to speak, the good place become bad place, a place to which men are drawn, but a place to be endured rather than enjoyed. An element of masochism enters the modernist notion of transcendence; but secular pessimism goes so far as to doubt whether the masochistic utopia can be attained, let alone sustained. In modernism it may seem—at least to the uninitiated—distinctly better to travel than to arrive: but the informed almost deny that the destination can be reached.

This descendentalism falls into two stages, the latter of which may either succeed and exclude the former or exist together with it in parallel or in combination.

The first of these stages is an eschatological descendentalism in which the romantic secular heaven becomes the modernist secular hell. The antithesis between this alienated world, this alienated self, and the other world of secular goodness and happiness is converted into the antithesis which opposes to degraded self and world another world—of greatness, yet of torment and suffering. From that other world stems the eschatological violence of so much modernism: the madness, the monstrousness, the infernal torture, the cosmological terror.

The second or epistemological stage of descendentalism is no less devoted to torment and suffering, but tends to abandon fantastic eschatological detail for a concern with this world only, whose significance it seeks to comprehend. Epistemological descendentalism withdraws from the celestial, and infernal, regions to matter of fact; it presumes that, in a world of universal evil, no other realm can or need be sought but that in which man comes to know the evil which is his life.

Modernists pessimistically doubt whether such knowledge is possible. Yet, in the phase of epistemological descendentalism, they do seek to understand the present order, and ordinary life, rather than that other, surreal order, that nightmare life, acknowledged by eschatological descendentalism. In contrast both to romantics and the modernists of that earlier phase, epistemological descendentalists take a new interest in the things of this world, if an interest expressed in terms of the greatest austerity.

## *The triumph of philistinism*

'*Philistinism!*' writes Arnold, '— we have not the expression in English. Perhaps we have not the word because we have so much of the thing.' The *word*, in its modern sense, originates from the jargon of German university students who called their enemies (and creditors) among the townsmen, *philistines*. Thereafter the term was adopted by romantics such as Hoffmann or Marx who used it to describe the urban many, equated first with the legal-administrative bourgeoisie and, later, with the commercial classes.

The *thing* is of course alienated man who, as romantic and modernist critics understand him, is so devoted to his alienated condition that he bends all his efforts to protect it, above all by imitating attempts to annul it. In short, he converts to the service of alienation all that properly belongs to the transcendence of alienation. Philistines specialise in what Arnold calls 'the grand name without the grand thing'; and the grand name that they purvey is borrowed from the transcendental. While genius offers us transcendental love or transcendental art, the estranged and estranging world proffers philistine love, philistine art, and so on.

The secular era has been interpreted, by its critics, as an uninterrupted substitution of the philistine for the transcendental. No system of government or society is likely to satisfy these critics. Yet systems which seek unity rather than multiplicity must come closest to realising the transcendental aspirations embodied in the concept of the one: and many such systems have been superseded or destroyed.

When the British rejected absolutism in the seventeenth century, they committed themselves to pluralist doctrines—liberal, democratic and commercial—which the world's critics ultimately found even more offensive than the doctrines of absolutism. During the eighteenth and nineteenth centuries, British imperial expansion, and Anglo-American technical and industrial innovations, gave those who held such doctrines, first in the United Kingdom and then in the United States, a pre-eminence and power greater than that enjoyed either by adherents to the absolutist tradition, or by admirers of the totalitarian principles of absolutism's continental critics.

In a decisive series of wars, the so-called 'Anglo-Saxons' not merely protected their own social systems but required both Japan and most of western Europe at least to pay lip service to the moral superiority of those systems. Meanwhile British and American economic, scientific and technological predominance long assured the credibility of Anglo-American doctrines over most of the globe. So that which eighteenth- and early nineteenth-century theorists abhorred in Britain and America as forces and notions inescapably tending to a human alienation ever more profound, have triumphed throughout the world.

Contrary forces and notions persist. Neither France nor Germany, for example, seem entirely to have accepted the Anglo-American tradition; and what is true in this respect of countries such as these is presumably the more true of a country such as Japan. Moreover the tradition whose transcendental aspirations were so thoroughly disappointed, both by absolutism and by British constitutionalism, has found vigorous support in modern totalitarian states of which no doubt the Soviet Union is the most important.

It might be thought, therefore, that those who argue that the principle of multiplicity fundamental to the Anglo-American tradition is the cause of man's alienated condition, could take comfort from the persistence of social and political elements, whole regimes even, committed to the counter-principle of unity. But this is not so.

For both liberal democrats and many of their enemies tend to group most advanced countries indiscriminately together as 'the rich nations', or 'late industrial societies', and to argue that these countries are 'converging' towards one pattern of consumption, expectations and assumptions, no part of which could be termed transcendental.

What kind of society is it that has proved so successful in the contemporary world, and towards which so much of the contemporary world is thought to be converging? It is a society characterised by what Ortega y Gasset, in his book *The Revolt of the Masses*, called a 'plenitude' of men and resources. The 'agglomeration' of population, the fact that humanity is now numerically many *more*, has important consequences for each individual.

'What previously was, in general, no problem',

observes Ortega, 'now begins to be an everyday one, namely, to find room.' And, as his acts and thoughts are reiterated by an ever greater number of fellows, each individual who seeks to 'find room' looks ever more like a uniform unit of an inhuman series.

Plenitude of wealth matches plenitude of numbers. 'Mass-man', who inhabits this multitudinous society, is, Ortega alleges, 'the spoiled child of human history'. Such a man, claims Ortega, has 'an inborn root-impression that life is easy, plentiful, without any grave limitations'. Indeed he 'finds within himself a sensation of power and triumph which invites him to stand up for himself as he is, to look upon his moral and intellectual endowment as excellent, complete.'

Whether or not citizens of advanced countries have a 'right' to the standards of life which they enjoy, those standards are desired by many, dissimilarly situated, who, by comparison with their own conditions, would agree with Ortega's description of those standards. Moreover those standards do affect the attitudes of those who do enjoy them: not least by encouraging a basic contentment with oneself as one is, especially in one's moral and cultural existence. Yet the human characteristics which caused generations of critics to describe men as alienated, persist in such a life of 'plenitude'.

For democratic and totalitarian societies display intense sectional conflict which fragments almost every aspect of these societies. It is true that democratic societies seek to contain this conflict within a prudential doctrine of 'majority rule'; and that, in order to justify their pretentious unitary claims, totalitarian societies deny that such conflict exists. But this fragmentation does exist—and produces precisely the multiplicity to which theorists from Rousseau onwards have attributed man's dehumanisation. This fragmentation enters the very individuality of man, who appears in modern societies only as the actor of many impersonal functional roles—employee, for example, consumer, voter, or patient. Thus men are not merely estranged from other men but divided and alienated within their own personality.

Man so existing prospers, however—by any standards but his own—and, though he frequently complains that he is hard up and hard done by, he would not change his lot for any other. He is, to adopt the terminology analysed in this book, a philistine, and his is naturally a philistine culture, which congratulates and justifies him.

The weakness of certain defences, or mitigations, of modern society is apparent. Yet mankind, having suffered a continuous critique of the very basis of its existence, and having endured the most varied exhortations to raise itself to higher things, has ignored both critique and exhortations, and established itself in the fullness and permanence of what that critique defines as triumphant philistinism.

Should the critique of philistinism be allowed any force—and clearly it has some—the triumph of philistinism poses exceedingly serious problems, to which the transition from romanticism to modernism is, in part, a response. That transition produces a culture which condemns—not pities—mankind's present condition because, even though what men are and do always falls short of what they could be and do, they are content with their lot. In short, modernists claim, men always prefer pushpin to poetry—indeed, always turn poetry into pushpin.

If modernists are right, some new attempt upon the transcendental (or descendental) would seem the only course conformable with the demands of human existence. If modernists were wrong, certain other conclusions would naturally follow. Yet such conclusions may seem scarcely to need investigation because, whatever the scepticism with which a few react to modernism, modernist culture fascinates the generality of men, and especially the generality of thinking men, in however philistine a fashion.

Says Mr Best in *Ulysses*, 'Mallarmé, don't you know . . . has written those wonderful prose poems. . . . The one about *Hamlet*. He says: *Il se promène, lisant au livre de lui-même*, don't you know, *reading the book of himself*.' Now the generality of men assume that a man may turn from the woeful world to literature and, by '*reading the book of himself*', may discover the transcendental significance of what would otherwise be mere life. Kafka, for example, is widely agreed to present a terrifying, but terrifyingly accurate, picture of contemporary man; and whoever so interprets such an author is very likely to read his work as a '*book of himself*' a book in which, for instance, Kafka's Josef K is the reader, and the court is the reader's world.

A reader of this sort is inclined to accept, perhaps

unconsciously, such an author's critique and transcendental aspirations. He is very likely to acquiesce in the author's evaluation of contemporary man and to acknowledge the justice of demands for genius—himself perhaps—to put an end to that man and make a new man in his stead. He acts, in short, as if he were the true reader for whom the work was written.

But that he cannot be if he is indeed simply an ordinary individual from among the generality of men. The book read by that individual, as we know him, meet him and are him—be that book any romantic or modernist work—is not 'the book of himself' but the book of genius. For the truth of the matter is that the philistines are ourselves, that we are the many, and that what we find in romantic and modernist literature is not ourselves but the one, the genius, manifest in the form of hero or martyr, or disguised as anti-heroic victim, in the form of the philistine many. Thus whether the modernist critique is correct or incorrect, it is a critique foreign to us, a critique meant not so much to expose a world in which we have no part as to reveal a world which has alienated us from real humanity, yet to which we owe the deepest, philistine devotion.

Our task might be to throw off our philistine habits and loyalties, to surrender ourselves into the hands of genius and to trust that the one may indeed save the many: and no doubt, in modernist eyes, that is to be our task, if we prove capable of it. Yet, in practice, remarkably few seem to have learned the real substance of this existential task; for strikingly many read

Kafka on Sundays and remain philistines throughout the week.

There may be no excuse for such behaviour. But there is every reason to suppose that the philistines will persist, and that we ourselves will still be numbered among them; and amid the criticism of ourselves which will also persist, it might be considered whether any justification can be offered for philistinism.

Such justification could be drawn directly from the ideology of genius itself. It is not simply that this ideology requires genius—and that behind each genius there must be a philistine also, either breeding or provoking him—but that the history of this ideology shows the very logic and tendency of philistinism to be the same as the logic and tendency of genius.

According to this ideology, genius transcends the alienated condition of the philistine many by introducing a higher or other order; and this order has been successively interpreted as the romantic transcendental and the eschatological, and then the epistemological descendental. In other words, genius has sought first a secular heaven, then a secular hell, and now the secular world, agreed perhaps to be in some sense hell, but allowed to be the world nevertheless. An everchanging genius has thus finally called men away from all other worlds, both good and bad, and concentrated their minds upon this world—admitted to be bad.

Philistinism has achieved the same end. For philistine degradation and vulgarisation has steadily reduced the transcendental to the this-worldly affairs of earth. Of course modernists hold that philistinism creates simply a realm of mere life (which it occupies incomprehendingly) while the genius establishes a realm of significance. Yet that distinction may be unreal, because modernist culture understands the significance of life to be little more than nonsignificance. Philistine incomprehension therefore seems to fall not far short of all the meaning that life has to offer. And if so, then philistinism would prove itself, by its results, to be genius.

## Culture without genius

Almost from the very beginning, romantics divided the concept of genius into two categories: that of the hero who triumphs immediately and directly over the forces of alienation; and that of the martyr who triumphs, but only through suffering and defeat. But secular culture's critical and pessimistic tendencies, the difficulties of attaining to the transcendental, and philistine opposition to the transcendental enterprise, soon concentrated romantic thought first on the category of the martyr, and then on that of the victim, who is at least *almost* denied his victory by the opposition of the many, the power of the estranging world, and the elusiveness of the transcendental.

Meanwhile the concept of genius underwent a further development. Religious culture dissociates the transcendental from evil, and presumes a heaven which is an absolute and unmixed good. Secular culture denies itself this notion, and tends to assume that evil is universal. Even in romanticism, where this tendency is by no means fully worked out, the transcendental can become morally ambiguous, and the genius demonic.

Modern culture's demonic vision has been embodied not merely in various rulers and artists of the romantic period but also in certain more recent historical figures, about whose personage clings a transcendental (or descendental) atmosphere inescapably the work of a long line of critics and visionaries. Genius has been conceived as the saviour of alienated man; and at various points during this century, genius has stepped out of the pages of literature to introduce, in the realm of politics, a new, a higher order. Whether this historical genius has appeared as hero, martyr, or victim, his efforts have been highly inimical to the well-being of the philistine many, not least in such matters as bread, life, and collective sanity.

Such depredations are not difficult to justify, given the ideology of genius. For according to that ideology, the genius, devoted to one transcendental aim, must, in Hegel's words, 'treat other great, even sacred, interests lightly ... trample many an innocent flower, crush many a thing in its way.' But it is not easy to see why such a justification should commend itself to the many, especially when, though flowers, innocent or otherwise, have been trampled in profusion, the transcendental obstinately fails to realise itself.

Thus the many might be allowed to withdraw—

with philistine indifference to niceties of discrimination—some or all of their confidence in modern culture; and it might be considered, strictly from the standpoint of philistine self-interest, whether culture might not do better without genius.

If culture without genius were agreed to be a project worth venturing upon, then that culture would most probably have first to be sought in a reinterpretation of the character of thinker or artist himself. W. H. Auden's largely Kierkegaardian study *The Enchafèd Flood* indicates some problems of such a reinterpretation. Auden describes genius as 'the religious hero' committed, with 'absolute passion', to 'the absolute truth, his god'. The religious hero can be represented as 'the nomad wanderer through the desert or over the ocean': though since genius is a progressive figure, his travels through these estranging realms must be presumed to have a destination, at which (romantics would hold) he arrives. But the 'heroic image' of such a traveller should now be reshaped, Auden suggests, as 'the less exciting figure of the builder, who renews the ruined walls of the city.'

Thinker or artist is rediscovered as the artificer who causes changes so modest and so limited that he signifies conservation rather than progress. Such a 'builder' 'renews the ruined walls': he re-does work that will not stand. Yet what he makes is neither the everlasting new Jerusalem, nor Mecca the nomad's goal, but simply the human city—which, too, in the end will not stand and must ever be renewed.

The artificer, the builder, is a mere craftsman. Even

as craftsman he is inferior to the genius, who is himself a technician of no mean order. For the artificer uses his skill to solve the problem itself.

E. H. Gombrich has often argued, and especially in an essay called 'The Renaissance Conception of Artistic Progress and its Consequences', that the 'mentality engendered by the idea of progress' issues in a concern with 'demonstrations of skill' in and for themselves. The works of an artist bent upon such displays 'exist not only for their own sake but also to demonstrate certain problem-solutions.'

So genius applies his technical skill to transcendental ends; he seeks to conquer those human estrangements from power which are the 'problems' that he solves. The artificer, on the contrary, is fundamentally concerned with *subjects*, not *problems*. He has tasks set him and fulfils those tasks by the most appropriate, and not the most difficult, methods. He builds walls; but he builds them from the ground up, not cantilevered out over space.

Genius's task arises from his drive to transcend men's alienated condition. 'The artist who believes that the arts progress', argues Gombrich, 'is automatically taken out of the social nexus of buying and selling' —that estranging bourgeois normality—and has to think 'not only of his commission but of his mission', his transcendental purpose.

But the artificer's tasks are laid upon him by the society that made him, and the culture that informs his work, even though both society and culture are alienated and alienating. While genius goes beyond society and annuls it in a higher order, the artificer works within the 'social nexus'; and his 'commission' is all-important. Whereas employment is ultimately impossible for genius, it is the social basis of the artificer's production, because that production serves to sustain a culture, and must therefore sustain the society (however alienating it may be held to be) which shapes and is shaped by that culture.

Moreover, genius is singlemindedly dedicated to his task and must oppose the alienation apparently implicit in any cultural activity. In that alienation, what was unitary man becomes, for example, 'writer', what was his unified thought becomes 'book'; and the writer and the book may well be appropriated to social or cultural ends other than the ends of genius.

The artificer encounters no such difficulties. He is required simply to use his specialised skill: he does his job, takes his pay and gets home. He neither desires to be joined to his work in transcendental unity nor understands his work as one work: on the contrary, his work is merely an employment divided into different commissions, different tasks.

We seem unlikely to reinterpret the artist as artificer. The concept of the artificer implies conservation, stability, and modern enthusiasm for progress is almost undiminished. Emphasis on subject matter, rather than form or 'problem', does not commend itself to present-day opinion. Above all, the idea of the artificer, and his employment by society, presupposes due machinery and due standards of commission not widely acknowledged to be feasible in a world where values are always in question, and where the resources to procure and facilitate cultural production are largely deemed to be in the wrong hands. Yet if genius is agreed to constitute an abnormality, a danger even, the many must either continue to seek culture from their enemy, or from philistine pseudo-genius, or must contrive to have it created by those able to realise the idea of artist as artificer.

## *Alienation and democracy*

If genius is removed from art at the same time as the artist is denied the claim to be a genius, art and indeed all culture, ceases to be transcendental and can be assessed only in this-worldly terms. Culture without genius might therefore be understood simply as entertainment. For a repudiation of the aspirations expressed in the ideology of genius might suggest that the most honest, the most satisfactory culture would be a purely instrumental culture designed to supply various convenient gratifications.

So baldly functional a culture would shun all else in order the more effectively to ease man's passage from cradle to grave. After all, given human self-consciousness, there is a problem of how to occupy the mind between inception and extinction, which problem culture—Eliot's catalogue of dog racing, Elgar, pickled beetroot, and the rest—is well suited to solve.

Yet culture so situated could be allowed another

role, close to that of religious culture in religious society. For religious culture, though transcendental in the sense that it turned men's eyes to heaven and to God, was profoundly this-worldly in the sense that it served to maintain a religious cult which took place, and religious doctrine taught and held, here on earth.

Secular culture lacks even the secular equivalent of this second function of religious culture; has remained absolutely committed to the secular transcendental; and has failed (except in philistine perversions) to sustain secular society's procedures, principles and norms. On the contrary, it ever criticises those procedures, principles and norms. But once and if secular culture could modify its loyalties to the transcendental, it should be free to sustain secular society and its values more thoroughly than religious culture once sustained a religious cult and its values.

Secular culture's failure to sustain society's fundamental values arises both from its presumption that society is alienated, and from the conviction that this alienated order could and would be transcended. Culture without genius denies that the alienated order can be transcended; and it might also assert that the this-worldly order is neither alienated nor alienating. But that assertion would merely substitute for doctrinaire absolute criticism an equally doctrinaire acceptance of the present order, worthy of philistinism at its worst.

Walter Kaufmann's recent essay, 'The Inevitability

of Alienation', indicates another possibility for a culture which rejected both absolute criticism and transcendental claims. Kaufmann believes that 'alienation is a central feature of human existence', and that 'as freedom, education, and self-consciousness increase, alienation grows too.' Kaufmann even argues—presumably because he finds alienation inseparable from freedom, education, and self-consciousness—that 'Life without estrangement is scarcely worth living'. But he admits that this situation raises problems and agrees that 'what matters is to increase men's capacity to cope with alienation.'

Kaufmann's views resemble those of certain romantics who attribute alienation to man's real and necessary development from the unalienated, naïve state; who interpret the contemporary human condition not merely as an advance on, but also as a decline from, the past; and who hope that future men will preserve and indeed continue their development while transcending their alienation.

Since Kaufmann holds alienation to be inevitable, he excludes the transcendental. But he agrees with the romantics that alienation is both good and evil. Alienation is a good, Kaufmann and the romantics argue, insofar as it represents, or at least is inseparable from, the development of mankind. Alienation is an evil, according to the romantics because it constitutes a degradation that must be transcended; and according to Kaufmann because it forms a disability that must be coped with.

Kaufmann adopts more or less the position which

would be taken by a culture that rejected transcendentalism and absolute criticism. By definition, such a culture cannot accept the final historical stage outlined by romantic theory, and must expect alienation to continue. How that culture would judge alienation is not so certain. It might completely reverse the doctrines of earlier secular culture and affirm the virtues of alienation as, in places, Kaufmann seems to do; it might assert that alienation is a necessary evil and address itself to manage or mitigate that evil.

In either eventuality, culture without genius must accept alienation as a characteristic, or the characteristic, of human life; and in both eventualities, such culture concerns itself with the social order, either by asserting the virtues of an alienation inseparable from society, or by treating of society's need to cope with the necessary evil of alienation. Thus, culture without genius would be a social culture which rejected the supra-social tendencies of transcendentalism and the anti-social activities of genius; and such a culture's subject matter—alienation and its virtues, alienation and its management, for example—is indeed suitable to a social culture.

If culture becomes social culture, affirms social values—at the very least by reckoning with, rather than repudiating, the alienated and alienating condition of society—then democracy must be the society most congruent with such a culture. For democracy is alienation fully realised: and, therefore, if culture comes to celebrate alienation as a good, democracy must be that culture's social ideal; while if culture comes to treat of alienation as humanity's lot, democracy will afford that culture's prime material.

Since a culture of the former type would be no less doctrinaire than culture shaped by the ideology of genius, the latter possibility seems to offer the more satisfactory option for a culture which excluded the transcendental. Given this option, culture's task is, in Kaufmann's phrase, to 'cope with' alienation and, in particular, to cope with alienation as it reveals itself in democracy.

Culture so interpreted must enable men to live as best they may within the ineluctable modality of their existence. What in the alienated condition is inhuman and inescapable must be recognised as such, what offers men the fullest possible humanity must be exploited. In this way, if the presuppositions of culture without genius be allowed, man may learn, through a culture and a society which reinforce each other, to achieve what he can of the hypothetical one, to accept what he must of the actual many. Whitman's words,

> One's self I sing, a simple separate person,
> Yet utter the word Democratic, the word En-masse

prefigure the difficulty which confronts a truly social culture.

Such a culture could not prescribe social forms or social roles in any didactic sense. Rather, by approaching society free from the absolute critical tendencies of romantics and modernists, and from the philistine pseudo-critical tendencies derived therefrom, this culture must be presumed to deal openly and directly with the great problems of society: namely, the relationship of individual and mass, and the future, in society, of individuals themselves.

These problems have found many solutions in the last two hundred years. Yet these solutions have been, in general, solutions to be imposed by the 'outstanding individual' on 'the individuals in the mass', in Kierkegaard's terminology. The mass has been required to be reconstituted from without, so to speak, as links in a chain, or parts of a harmonious organic whole. It would be a mark of social culture to create those intellectual, emotional and spiritual conditions in which the individuals in the mass might resolve their own problems themselves.

Though Mill seemed to assent to the doctrine of Humboldt that 'the end of man' was 'the highest and most harmonious development of his powers', the completed 'individuality of' his 'power and development', he wished to show that these great human objects could be achieved by reducing social control to the bare minimum necessary to enable the free and unhindered development of individuals. That minimum role is obviously a dangerous role for society. But it is a role to which liberal democratic society ever seeks to tend, however ineffectually, and it is a role which can give great scope to a culture that serves both to situate individuals in a minimal social environment, to mediate society's existence to them, and to generate the materials with which individuals can develop their own powers, their own individuality.

However it be interpreted, a social culture is clearly

a this-worldly culture which neither condemns the world as absolute evil nor relies upon the promise of another and better world. Such a culture contents itself with what it has, and does not look beyond to something other. It thus succeeds *both* to the ideology of genius, which—through the stages of romantic transcendentalism, and eschatological and epistemological descendentalism—shifted men's attention from another world to this, *and* to the concomitant philistinism which called everything down to earth with a historically decisive efficiency.

That fact reemphasises democracy's association with such a culture. For democratic thought is based upon the rationalist empiricist principle that science, or common sense, discovers all there is, and there is no 'reality' other than the 'appearances' so discovered. Hence when culture commits itself to appearances, to phenomena, it assents to democratic intellectual method, and no doubt gives its assent with an enthusiasm unshared by certain earlier cultural movements in the history of democratic countries.

A culture of 'appearances', which rejects the possibility of immanent or transcendent reality, necessarily involves itself in some affirmation, some acceptance of this apparent world, however qualified. But altogether to reject the other, allegedly real world, and altogether to be involved in this world, is an almost impossible position. Joyce, for example, sought to affirm the world and, in certain ways, to accept it. In some respects, therefore, he moved towards a social, a non-transcendental culture of the type here considered.

Yet Joyce is a writer adapted far better to illustrate the difficulties, than to display the potentialities, of this type of culture.

Joyce's affirmation and acceptance of the apparent or the phenomenal world can be seen in those passages in his essay on James Clarence Mangan, and in *Stephen Hero*, where he contrasted what he called the 'romantic' and the 'classical temper'. The transcendental, romantic temper, according to Joyce, finds 'no fit abode here for its ideals'. The classical temper, on the contrary, 'ever mindful of limitations, chooses rather to bend upon these present things . . .' because 'so long as this place in nature is given us it is right that art should do no violence to the gift.'

The classical temper, bending upon these present things, might seem a genuine acceptance of the alienated order—which nevertheless does not deny that order's alienation—such as has here been attributed to the notion of culture without genius, or of a social culture. But this is not so; and the sense in which it is not so may show the difference between what Joyce achieved in his definition and what is here envisaged.

For while Joyce requires his classical temper to 'bend upon these present things', he expects the classical temper so to 'work upon' and 'fashion' these present things 'that the quick intelligence may go beyond them to their meaning which is still unuttered.' The classical temper, while drawing closer to these present alienated and alienating things than ever romanticism was able to do, still uses them to evoke their mysterious, transcendental, unuttered meaning.

A truly new understanding of alienation, a truly this-worldly culture would not merely bend upon but stick at these present things: neither abstracting them into transcendental art, like Schopenhauer, nor going beyond them to their transcendental meaning, like Joyce, but accepting them, seriously and critically, as the inescapable phenomena of a world permanently alienated.